BOUND IN SILENCE

An Unsolved Murder in a Small Texas Town

CHRISTENA STEPHENS

STONEY CREEK PUBLISHING
www.stoneycreekpublishing.com

Published by
Stoney Creek Publishing
stoneycreekpublishing.com

Copyright © 2023 by Christena Stephens
Distributed by Texas A&M University Press

ISBN: 979-8-9879002-0-8
ISBN (ebook): 979-8-9879002-1-5
Library of Congress: 2023920656
Second Printing

Cover & interior design by Monica Thomas for
TLC Book Design, *TLCBookDesign.com*

Cover images:
top image *Lubbock Avalanche*—Journal Archives
bottom image Adobestock © jacky lam/EyeEm

Printed in the United States

*"Evidence always bears the mark of
the personality of the person who gathers
it just as truly as does the honey
smell of the bee."*

–WILLIAM WADSWORTH, 1915

"Not Our Doctor Roy— And His Wife, Too!"

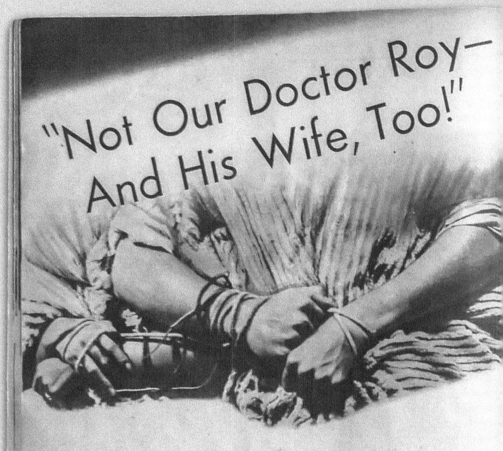

All Littlefield, Texas, Loved This Popular Young Doctor. Yet Somebody Tortured Him and His Pretty Wife to Death. Why? How Find the Murderer?

By Herbert Mason

Special Investigator for
ACTUAL DETECTIVE STORIES

BIG, burly Sam Hutson smelled the sickening odor the minute he stepped into the dark room. It was faint. But it was there. And he was struck with its terrible sweetness.

Hutson stepped into the living-room. The place was quiet. The venetian blinds were drawn, letting in little light. A cool north wind, sweeping down across the Texas Panhandle, whipped through the open front door of the Doctor Roy E. Hunt home that Tuesday morning of October 26, 1943.

Just behind the Sheriff was his deputy, Sid Topping, and the Littlefield, Texas, Police Chief, Ab Anderson. Littlefield's night patrolman, J. L. Walters, remained outside the home to hold back the crowd. The news was spreading rapidly through that city that "our Doctor Hunt" and his wife have been murdered." It was always "our" Doctor Hunt. For the people loved this young doctor who had taken

out the children's tonsils, nursed their colds and bruises, delivered their babies and listened to their troubles.

Now he had been murdered. He and his sweet, tiny wife. And the Doctor's neighbors were "damn mad Texans."

Sheriff Hutson stopped suddenly. From a room at the back of the tan, brick house had come a child's frightened cry.

"Mommy! Mommy!"

Deputy Topping hurried through the dinette, the small hallway and into the back bedroom. A moment later he returned with a small girl, about three years old. She was dressed in a pink nightgown. Her face was stained with tears. She looked at the officers, frightened.

"Mommy!" she cried out again.

"I'll take her over to the neighbor's home where the other daughter is," Topping said. And he hurried out.

Sheriff Hutson stepped gingerly

through the door at his left, and into the main bedroom. He paused for a moment, staring at the bloody and horrible scene before him.

Doctor Hunt and his wife lay side by side in the bed. The Doctor had been shot between the eyes. Blood had poured from the hole and made a small rivulet across his cheek and neck. His eyes were wide and staring now, as if he had died looking at a ghost.

THE only blood on Mrs. Hunt seemed to have spattered from her husband. She looked so quiet and peaceful, as if she were sleeping. A big, swollen mark showed on the center of her forehead, but the skin wasn't broken. Hutson started to feel for the woman's pulse, but he stopped the minute his hand touched her flesh. No use probing for a pulse beat in that cold wrist.

Hunt's jaw had twisted at a strange angle—as if he had been hit a terrific

10

This is the layout of the Hunt home, tracing the movements of the killer and of one of the Doctor's children. Police had to know every detail before they could even hope to trap the wily murderer

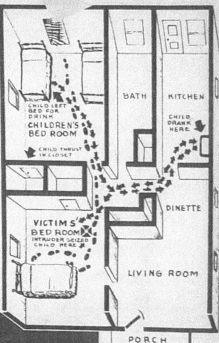

jolt. Both bodies were still completely clothed.

A belt, wire coat hangers, string, rope, lamp cord and a woman's under garments had been used to tie the bodies tightly together. Mrs. Hunt had been gagged with a handkerchief.

The room didn't seem to be disturbed. The killer apparently had come into the house, quietly went about his business of killing the couple, then calmly departed. But why?

On the floor of the bedroom Hutson noticed muddy footprints. It had rained the night before. The killer probably had left those prints. Hutson followed the trail into the back bedroom where the Hunts' two daughters, and only children, Jo Ann, six, and Jane, three, had slept the night before.

THEN Hutson saw how the killer had entered the house. The back bedroom window was open, the venetian blind twisted and broken. Hutson looked out the window. Footprints on the sill indicated that the murderer had crawled through the window. Just underneath the sill was one of the Hunt girls' small chairs. The killer had stood on it as he climbed up or down.

Hutson looked at that chair a minute. Without realising it, he spoke aloud the thoughts that were in his mind. "Wonder why he used that chair. It would have been a lot more simple to crawl in the window without it."

Being careful not to touch anything that might be smeared with a tell-tale fingerprint, Hutson hurried back into the front bedroom.

"You stay here, Ab," he told the Police Chief. "Look around and see what you can find. Don't let anybody in. I'm going to call the Rangers, get Maney Gault up here. And I want to have a talk with little Jo Ann."

When Hutson walked outside, Patrolman Walraven was having trouble with the crowd that had gathered around the Hunt home, demanding angrily to be told what was going on.

HUTSON spoke sharply. "You people go back home. I'm Sheriff here, and I've never let you down yet. I won't now. We'll get whoever did this. But you're surely not helping us any standing around here getting in the way. When we want to see you, we'll come to you. Then you can help us in every way possible."

The people grew calm. Slowly, one by one, they started walking away, talking in hushed, menacing tones.

Hutson noticed how fresh and clean the outside air smelled. The odor inside the house! That was why it seemed so good to be outdoors. What was that odor? He'd never smelled it before. It was something like a hospital. Maybe, Hutson assured himself, the odor was there just because it was a doctor's house.

Sheriff Hutson walked down the street to the home of Mr. and Mrs. L. C. Grissom. It was there that the Hunts' two children had been taken after this morning's shocking tragedy. The Grissoms and the Hunts had been friends for several years, Hutson knew.

When Grissom admitted the Sheriff into his home, Hutson took one look around the room. His glance stopped

[floor plan labels:]
CHILD LEFT BED FOR DRINK
CHILDREN'S BED ROOM
CHILD THRUST IN CLOSET
VICTIMS' BED ROOM
INTRUDER SEIZED CHILD HERE
BATH
KITCHEN
CHILD DRANK HERE
DINETTE
LIVING ROOM
PORCH

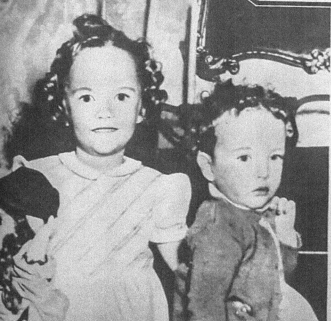

Jo Ann Hunt, left, shown with her sister Jane, said the ugly man looked like a monster

suddenly. He saw what he was looking for. The two Hunt girls were huddled on the sofa in Mrs. Grissom's arms. Both looked like frightened animals. Instinctively they drew closer to Mrs. Grissom when they saw Hutson.

But, in his rough way, which was nevertheless genuine and warm, Hutson soon made friends with the Hunt children, and five minutes later he was able to ask Jo Ann simple questions and get the whole story from her.

"WHAT were your mother and father doing last night when you went to sleep?" he asked her.

"They—they were playing cards," the child replied slowly, hesitantly.

"Were they alone?"

Jo Ann shook her head vigorously. "Doctor James was there, and his wife, and Mr. Gradbury was there, too."

Hutson knew these people.

"Did you and Jane go right to sleep?"

The child nodded.

"And what happened after that?"

"I—I woke up and I was thirsty and I went to the kitchen to get a drink of water. I smelled something funny. Then I thought I heard somebody in Mommy's room." The child's lip

31

For all the girls and women
whose voices have
been silenced.

CONTENTS

INTRODUCTION

The best nonfiction stories are rarely tidy or perfect. Imagine the messiest desk you have ever seen and multiply it visually by one hundred. Amongst all the stacks of paper, chaos is where the truth of the story lies. Or it may not lie. But the story itself becomes a series of tied ropes linking together throughout each chapter.

This nonfiction historical narrative started with seeing a faded black and white newspaper photograph dated October 26, 1943. That image led to desks, floors, and tables being covered in papers. Then came the unsettling dreams I had during this research. Both were leading me down a path I thought I would never take.

Historical research and dreams are not supposed to correlate in any way. Dreams are the stories our brains tell while we are sleeping. Historical research involves countless hours of poring through old books, journals, and newspapers. This book is how both came together.

Then I reflect on what came next, which was the often-asked question, "Why did you become interested in this murder story?" Naturally, people assumed a relation had to exist between me and the Hunt or Newton families.

No, all this began while searching for my family's history in aged, leather-bound issues of the Littlefield, Texas newspaper, *The County Wide News,* from the 1930s and 1940s.

The purpose of my searching for a news story dealt with a car wreck that left my dad handicapped and that almost killed all his paternal family, after a three-car head-on collision south of Amarillo, Texas on December 25th. According to the family story, the wreck threw my grandmother Christena, Uncle George, and Aunt Dorris from the car into a nearby field. My Aunt's leg was broken. My grandmother had been holding my three-week-old dad in her arms and was miraculously still clinging to him as she lay in the field. Two of my great uncles were in the car as well. The newspapers at that time left me hopeless for answers.

I continued scanning through the old newspaper issues, looking at early advertisements, and reading headlines about the humdrum life in rural towns. With one turn of a yellowed and fragile newspaper page, the routine world I became so familiar with page after page quavered by a murder headline. My eyes landed on the centered top-fold photograph and instantly it became fixed in my memory.

This five-by-seven photo featured two curly-haired young girls sitting in front of an upright piano. The oldest girl was smiling and holding on to a doll, with her other arm wrapped around the younger, wide-eyed girl. The caption read:

> "A bad man killed them," said little five-year-old Jo Ann Hunt, daughter of Dr. and Mrs. Roy E. Hunt, who were found murdered in their bed early Tuesday morning told neighbors and peace officers' after spending several hours sleeping in a clothes closet where she was shoved in by the murderer. Jo Ann holds her doll in one arm and tenderly puts her arm around her little sister, Jane, age 3."

The photo, with a passing glance, appeared to have been a family photo. It is evident neither child grasped the emblazoned headline and the consequences that had befallen them. Compelled to make copies of the articles, I later went to the Lamb County Courthouse to copy the court case files related to the murders.

Other life duties called, and I forgot about the documents I had copied until nearly twenty years later. During that intervening time, I dreamed about these murders more times than I can remember, as well as of the two girls in the photograph.

Those dreams and preliminary research lead me where I least expected—to a small southern Oklahoma town.

In January 2012, I sat at a small wooden dining table in an emblematical 1970s brick home in the Sooner state, which happened to belong to the oldest girl from the photo. Jo Ann Hunt had recounted the events the night her parents were murdered.

Our Oklahoma meeting resulted from a historical paper I presented in Lubbock, Texas. In the fall of 2008, I went through those initial copies I had made years before, and concluded I had enough material to present a ten-page paper to the West Texas Historical Association (WTHA) at its annual meeting held in April 2009 in Lubbock.

An article written about my forthcoming paper by *Lubbock Avalanche-Journal* features reporter Ray Westbrook drew one of the largest crowds ever for a historical presentation. Attendees included Sue Hunt Sexton and Bob Hunt, the niece and nephew of murder victim Dr. Roy Hunt.

During the presentation, you could hear a pin drop. The audience became hooked from the first word to the last. After I finished and sat down, Sue Hunt Sexton grabbed both my shoulders and buried her face into my hair, and through tears, she kept saying, "Thank you. Thank you." I had not expected any kind of reaction from anyone. For me, I was only presenting historical research on a double homicide.

Then another unexpected event occurred at this meeting. A fellow WTHA member, Gene Pruess, whom I had befriended while working on another historical research project, approached me and dropped this bomb, "I've got the original crime scene photos! They're yours if you want them and you should turn this into a book." I was speechless.

Researching and recounting the murders of Roy and Mae Hunt has not been easy. These murders are an unimaginable crime in any decade, and the task of writing about them became more challenging with all the twists and turns of the story that were discovered since my original WTHA presentation.

All my sources are from primary materials of court records, newspapers, and appeal trial transcripts. I also researched forensic techniques from published police journals, books on collecting crime scene evidence, and analysis techniques available in the 1940s.

This is a work of nonfiction. No names were changed, no characters invented, and no event fabricated. Quotes are from newspaper reports or trial transcripts, except for my interviews with Jo Ann Hunt.

As research reveals, most stories, like this one, typically produce more questions than answers. This research also revealed many ties to each character in this story are all connected in some form or another.

The Hunt murder story is important because it highlights turbulent events of the era with many disturbing twists that made this entire investigation into a shoddy, almost bullshit attempt to catch a murderer. More important, this book provides a key eyewitness account that the police never bothered to get—Jo Ann Hunt's. She was threatened into never talking about the murders and remained bound in silence for almost seventy years after her parents' deaths, even though the person who had threatened her had died years earlier. Children should never be silenced—especially when they endure trauma.

·•• KEY PLAYERS •·•

Hubert Deere — Oklahoma resident who murdered Jim Thomas

Benjamin Maney Gault — Texas Ranger

Baxter Honey — Lubbock, Texas retired police officer

George M. Hunt — Lubbock County, Texas Pioneer and grandfather of Dr. Roy Hunt

Jo Ann Hunt — Oldest daughter of Dr. Roy and Mae Hunt

Mae Franks Hunt — Wife of Dr. Roy Hunt who was murdered

Dr. Roy Hunt — Littlefield, Texas doctor who was murdered

Samuel (Sam) Hutson — Sheriff of Lamb County, Texas

Leroy Kelley — Convicted of killing Sheriff Franklin Loyd in 1937

Harold LaFont — Texas District Attorney for 64th Judicial District

Franklin Loyd — Sheriff of Lamb County, Texas from 1935–1937

Ruth Newton — Cameron, Texas resident and wife of Dr. Billy Newton

Dr. William (Billy) Newton — Cameron, Texas doctor accused and convicted of attempted murder of Roy Hunt

Clarence Russell — Texas 64th District Judge for the trials of Dr. Billy and Ruth Newton and Jim Thomas

Jim Thomas — Tried for the murder of Roy Hunt

·•• TIMELINE •••·

May 19, 1942: Phone calls began

May 20, 1942: Attempted murder of Dr. Roy Hunt

August 1942: Dr. Billy's and Ruth Newton's attempted murder of Dr. Roy Hunt trials are set and postponed

February 1943: Newtons' cases are placed again on the Lamb County docket

August 23, 1943: Dr. Billy and Ruth Newton's first trial in the attempted murder of Dr. Roy Hunt

August 26, 1943: Dr. Billy Newton convicted in the attempted murder of Dr. Roy Hunt and sentenced to seven years

October 26, 1943: Dr. Roy and Mae Hunt are murdered

November 15, 1943: Ruth Newton's case called in Lamb County for attempted murder of Dr. Roy Hunt

January 1944: Ruth Newton's case moved to Hale County

January 5, 1944: Dr. Billy Newton's first appeal filed

February 1944: Lamb County grand jury convenes for Hunt murders

March 15, 1944: Dr. Billy Newton appeal decision handed down, reversing the Lamb County conviction

April 10, 1944: Jim Thomas indicted of Dr. Roy Hunt's murder

June 1944: Ruth Newton's case set in Hale County for attempted murder of Dr. Roy Hunt

August 28, 1944: Jim Thomas's trial held in Hale County

August 30, 1944: Jim Thomas convicted of Dr. Roy Hunt's murder

September 25, 1944: Dr. Billy Newton's Hale County trial for attempted murder of Dr. Roy Hunt

October 5, 1944: Jury misconduct ruled in Jim Thomas's Hale County case

January 8, 1945: Jim Thomas's second trial held in Dawson County for murder of Dr. Roy Hunt

January 12, 1945: Jim Thomas found guilty of Dr. Roy Hunt's murder

May 8, 1945: Jim Thomas's first appeal is filed

October 3, 1945: Jim Thomas's first appeal decision handed down, reversing Dawson County conviction

June 1, 1946: Dr. Billy Newton's case set in Hale County for attempted murder of Dr. Roy Hunt

June 5, 1946: Dr. Billy Newton's Hale County verdict deadlocked

August 27, 1946: Jim Thomas's murder case moved from Dawson County to Nolan County

September 30, 1946: Dr. Billy Newton's attempted murder trial of Dr. Roy Hunt in Swisher County

October 4, 1946: Dr. Billy Newton convicted of assault with intent to murder in Swisher County, sentenced to two years

April 23, 1947: Dr. Billy Newton files second appeal

October 15, 1946: Jim Thomas's third trial set in Nolan County for the murder of Dr. Roy Hunt

October 19, 1946: Jim Thomas convicted in murder of Dr. Roy Hunt in Nolan County

February 18, 1947: Jim Thomas's second appeal filed for Nolan County conviction

June 28, 1947: Jim Thomas's appeal decision handed down, reversing Nolan County conviction

July 30, 1947: Dr. Billy Newton enters prison for attempted murder of Dr. Roy Hunt

July 12, 1948: Dr. Billy Newton released from prison

August 22, 1951: Jim Thomas killed in Durant, Oklahoma

November 1951: Hubert Deere's trial for the murder of Jim Thomas

January 8, 1953: Nolan County dismisses Jim Thomas's murder of Dr. Roy Hunt case

PROLOGUE

The car ride was soundless except for the rumble of the tire noise on the highway asphalt. In the back seat of the big black sedan, a five-year-old girl and her three-year-old sister were bundled in coats and hats. Miles and miles passed with unnatural quietness. There was nothing for them to look at along the way because the green grasses had already disappeared with the October cold nights, making everything a pale yellow.

By this late October 1943 day, the mesquite and soapberry and hackberry trees were barren of their leaves, making them silent sentinels to the coming days, months, and years for the girls. Not even the sun shined to illuminate the darkness inside the car as it drove on almost 200 miles east from Lubbock.

Arriving in Vernon, Texas, the woman sitting in the passenger seat escorted the girls into a large house, even grander than the home they were taken from. She led them to the bathroom and then to the kitchen for a drink and some food. Eventually, she steered them upstairs to the master bedroom.

As the oldest girl stood in the bedroom doorway holding her sister's hand, the woman settled into a rocking chair and motioned with an index finger. The girl let go of her sister's hand and gingerly approached the woman. Without a moment's hesitation, like a sudden

West Texas wind gust, the room turned bitter cold as the woman spoke sternly to the five-year-old girl, shaking her pointed index finger close to the child's face.

"You are never to talk about what happened in that house ever again, do you understand me? If you do, you will never see your sister ever again. I will separate you both forever!"

To make the point clearer, the woman repeated it again, this time shaking the young girl by the shoulders. Tears formed in the little girl's eyes as she leaned over to look past the woman at her sister.

Her heart raced. As soon as her eyes met her sister's, she knew instinctively she would never speak of what happened, of what she had seen, of the events that led them to this house, with the stern, cold woman. The only home they had ever known seemed a million miles away.

The voice of Jo Ann Hunt, Roy and Mae Hunt's oldest daughter, was silent for nearly seventy years after her parents' murders, even though the person who had threatened her had died years earlier.

Why was Jo Ann warned into silence over her parents' murders? This becomes the first question of this story.

In July 2010, I was honored to finally meet Roy and Mae Hunt's daughters. They traveled to Lubbock to personally meet me at the request of their cousin, Sue Sexton. The faded photograph that had become ingrained in my memory of them sitting in front of that upright piano came to life for me. Though aged due to the passage of time, I recognized Jo Ann and Jane instantaneously.

My own heart was racing as I sat on a floral sofa in Sue's living room with Jo Ann mere inches from me and Jane facing me on the opposite couch. The conversation started off light between us. Both Jo Ann and Jane settled my nerves quickly by asking a lot of questions about me, as well as the all-important question of why I was interested in this story.

With nerves calmed and hearts back to beating normally, Jo Ann soon told me that they had traveled to Littlefield the day before. This was the first and only time either of them had been back in Littlefield since their parents' murders. Jo Ann was immediately able to locate their childhood home, as well as the hospital their dad helped build. They shared more stories about the hospital than the house. They loved a fountain that had goldfish in it. They dropped in at the Duggan Museum and had an interesting encounter there with the curator. The sisters also visited their parents' gravesites in the Lubbock Cemetery.

Jo Ann moved along, sharing stories about her brief life in the bucolic West Texas town. She stated she was known as Littlefield's "Little Princess" because all the residents knew her. As an infant, electric lights were placed around her bassinet to keep her small, premature body warm. As a young child, she wore leg braces to correct her bow-leggedness. At some point later, she contracted ringworm because Jo Ann loved carrying her cat on top of her head. With the ringworm came a shaved head and she wore a knitted cap with braids to cover her baldness as her hair grew back. Like any young child from this regional farming community, Jo Ann's small hands even picked cotton.

She was forbidden by her mom to cross the street by herself in any direction. Often, especially if her mother had scolded her about something, Jo Ann would run to the end of the block and sit down on the corner waiting for people to come by so she could talk to them. It was as if she was "running away." She loved talking to the people across the street or even to the ones walking by her. This took me back to a time when the streets were a safe haven for kids because I could imagine her sitting on the corner of Seventh Street waving at people and her saying hi to them.

Jo Ann reminisced with bright eyes about visiting with the neighborhood families and making chocolate chip cookie mud pies. She used real sugar in those pies more than once, she said laughing, which got her into immense trouble with her momma. Hence the cause of her many times of 'running away.' Jo Ann remembered attending the small Methodist church down the street from their home with her parents. She specifically recalled participating in Vacation Bible School in the summer of 1943.

Jo Ann never spoke about her parents' murders, not even to Jane, until six months prior to my 2010 Lubbock meeting with them. Jane quickly interjected by raising her hand, affirming, "It was not until six months ago when Jo Ann started talking about the murders because she had been living with this lifelong threat."

Jo Ann's witness account of what occurred in her home on that fateful night is not what was reported in the court documents or the newspapers. Yes, Lamb County Sheriff Sam Hutson talked to her. Yes, she was brought into the courtrooms. But no one ever stopped long enough to talk to her on an eye-to-eye level, to ask Jo Ann what she saw in the house on the morning of the murders. It was always bits of information here and there, like the foremost assumption that she was placed in the nursery closet by the murderer. District Attorney Harold LaFont never even spoke to her until she appeared in the courtrooms.

The woman's threats took hold of her voice. Jo Ann did not speak about what happened in that house for seventy years. Her story is recorded here for the first and only time.

PART ONE

MURDERS

1

BROKEN SILENCE

Jo Ann's Account That Fateful Night

The tiny house was near capacity that night for games and dinner. From the radio, the voices and music of Bing Crosby, Tommy Dorsey, Benny Goodman, The Ink Spots, and likely Duke Ellington filled the house.

Mae Hunt put her girls to bed around 8:00 p.m., tucking them into their beds and gently kissing them goodnight. Both girls soon fell asleep with the hum of laughter going on inside the living room while guests enjoyed the evening eating Mae's cooking and playing card games.

Hours later, Jo Ann was startled awake and sat straight up in her bed. A scripture she had learned in Bible School was running through her head, Matthew 28:20: "Teaching them to observe all things whatsoever, I have commanded you: and lo, I am with you always, even unto the end of the world." Later, Jo Ann would come to believe she was awakened by the sound of a gunshot.

She glanced over at Jane, who was standing up in her crib. Jane pointed to the window and said, "Man." Jo Ann didn't understand what her little sister meant. Nor did she realize the window was open.

She needed to go to the bathroom, so she crawled out of her bed and walked into the small hallway.

She looked to her right and noticed her parents' south bedroom door was closed. Immediately, she knew something was not right. Her parents always kept their bedroom door open. They also left the bathroom light on, but now, it was off.

Jo Ann walked up to the bedroom door and knocked. With her face to the door, she said she had to go to the bathroom. A few seconds later, her mother, Mae, called out to her from the bedroom: "Do not open the door. I cannot go to the bathroom with you. You can go by yourself."

Jo Ann turned around, went to the bathroom, and then returned to bed. As she lay there in the near darkness, she kept hearing noises and sounds she had never heard before coming from her parents' bedroom. She crawled out of bed, tiptoed to the door, and knocked again. Mae called out to her, "Do not open the door!" Those were the last words her mother spoke to her.

Abruptly, the bedroom door swung open, and Jo Ann jumped in terror. Instead of her mom or dad, she saw a man wearing gloves and a mask. He stooped over and grabbed her by the shoulders, jostled her inside the bedroom, and shoved her into her parents' claustrophobic closet, shutting the door and encasing her in total darkness.

From within the tiny closet, no more than three feet from her parents' bed, Jo Ann could hear the man beating her mother, and she could hear her mother pleading with him over and over. To a five-year-old child, the sounds her mother kept making were indescribable, but Jo Ann understood enough to know something terrible was happening to her mother. She moved inside the closet, possibly making a noise. Moments later, the door opened, and the murderer threw a wet rag on top of her that smelled like gasoline. Overcome by the odor, she quickly passed out.

She awoke, still in the darkened closet. She listened carefully. Silence greeted her. She reached up and turned the doorknob, gently opened the door, and crept out of the closet as wisps of light creeped into the room. Jo Ann did not walk toward her parents' bed. She believes in that moment, God spoke to her again, telling her not to look at the bed. She opened the south bedroom door and tiptoed back to the nursery. She paused and noticed the kitchen door was closed. That, too, always remained open.

As she stepped into the nursery, she saw Jane standing in her crib. Jo Ann whispered to her sister to remain quiet. She lifted Jane out of her crib and put shoes and a coat on her. Then Jo Ann put her own coat and shoes on.

The nursery window was open. Jo Ann lifted Jane out of the window and lowered her down onto a little red chair below. Jo Ann then climbed out after her. Hand in hand, the girls walked in silence around the corner toward the front of the house.

As they reached the sidewalk, Jo Ann paused to look in both directions. To her right, she saw Mrs. Grissom putting her purse in her car. Jo Ann started crying and, tugging Jane, ran across the street toward the lady they barely knew.

Hearing the commotion, Mr. Grissom came out the house. Jo Ann tried to tell the Grissoms what happened, but they did not listen. They tried to take Jo Ann back to the house, but she fought them and refused. The Grissoms put her in a bed in their house. Then, Mrs. Grissom then carried Jane, who was not yet three, back into the Hunt home. Jane has no memory of that day.

Tied Together in Death

Hours earlier, as the October cold and darkness shrouded the town of Littlefield, in the Texas Panhandle, a killer picked up a child's red metal chair and positioned it under a nursery window on the backside of the Hunt's house on 7th street. Unlatching the window screen, he placed the chair against the wall and slowly raised the window—the same one Jo Ann and Jane would crawl through hours later.

The killer pulled up the blinds, and stepping on the chair, bent himself over to fit through the window. He paused, noticing the two young girls. One was awake. He silently proceeded to the bathroom, shut off the light, and entered Roy and Mae Hunt's bedroom, quietly closing both bedroom doors. With the couple still sleeping, he took out his gun and walked to the bed.

The noise awakened Roy and Mae. Immediately, the assailant hit Roy on the left side of his face, likely with the butt of the gun, bashing in his jaw and knocking him unconscious. The attacker swiftly pointed the gun at Mae, whispering to her to be quiet and not move. He then yanked the bedding off the couple and proceeded to bind Roy.

As Roy regained consciousness, he struggled against his bonds. Annoyed by the constant movements, the killer placed the barrel of the gun against Roy's forehead and pulled the trigger. Roy's life ended in seconds.

Mae screamed when the gun fired. The assailant hit her on the side of her head with the butt of his gun to silence her. As he struggled with Mae, he removed her panties and laid them around her neck. He held her down, arms above her head, using enough force to bruise her right arm. Then, most likely, he raped her.

In these terrifying moments, Mae heard Jo Ann calling from the other side of the bedroom door. Frightened for her daughters' lives, Mae pleaded with Jo Ann not to open it. A few minutes later, Jo Ann knocked again. Again, Mae implored her daughter to leave the door closed.

The murderer walked a few steps across the small room, opening the south bedroom door. He grabbed the child by her shoulders and pulled her into the bedroom, closing the door before throwing her into the closet. He returned to Mae and most likely gave her another blow to the head.

At some point, perhaps hearing a noise from the closet, he opened the closet door and threw a chloroformed rag over her head.

The killer returned to the bed, laying the Hunts side by side in their full-size bed. He bound the bloodied couple in a strange and detailed fashion. He tied Roy's right leg and Mae's left leg together with a wire coat hanger and a leather belt. He then took another small cord and tied it around Roy's neck, down around his arm, and through his wristwatch. Then, he ran the cord through Mae's wristwatch and up around her neck. He bound their arms together with another cord. Finally, he tied two of Roy's neckties around their necks.

Because of Mae's struggling, the killer hit her once more in the left temple, fracturing her skull and causing her to bleed internally. Before leaving, he placed a handkerchief across Mae's mouth and another under Roy's chin, and then another pair of Mae's panties. The killer left the bedroom, walked into the kitchen, shut the door. He hurried out of the house through the back door, breaking the backyard gate off its hinges as he fled.

Roy was thirty-five; Mae was twenty-six.

Immediately after Their Parents' Deaths

The hours after the bodies were discovered were like a West Texas whirlwind. The girls' uncle, Dr. Ewell Hunt, examined them at the Grissoms' home before they were taken to their paternal grandparents' home in Lubbock. According to Ewell, Jo Ann was lucky to have survived because of the high dose of chloroform she inhaled from the rag the killer threw over her head.

At their grandparents' house, a reporter later photographed the girls sitting in front of the family piano. It appeared on the front pages of newspapers across the country.

Mae's sister, Ruth Borchardt, took custody of the girls, as she had after the earlier incident in which Roy Hunt was shot and almost killed. Not much is known regarding the relationship of these sisters or what kind of person Ruth was. But after the murders, her threats to Jo Ann that she remain quiet intensified over the years.

Neither Roy's parents nor his brothers had a say in where the girls should stay. They all tried to keep them in Lubbock, but a judge granted full custody to Mae's sister.

Neither girl attended their parents' funeral.

After hours of silence in the car and their arrival at Ruth's house in Vernon, Ruth admonished Jo Ann to never speak of what had happened. Her parents' deaths were too sad to talk about. Her aunt emphasized the need for silence with a threat: if she ever mentioned the night her parents were killed, she would be sent away forever and never see Jane again. At five years old, Jo Ann believed her finger-pointing aunt and the threat she conveyed.

Fear of never seeing Jane again bound Jo Ann to silence. She became Jane's protector at a high cost to herself.

As the months turned into years, Jo Ann never talked about the murders, and neither did the Hunt family. Not even Mae's family, the Franks, mentioned the murders in the girls' presence. It was as if ignoring something made it seem less real, like it never happened.

No one asked Jo Ann to tell them what happened that night. In newspaper reports, the sheriff said he had talked with her, but Jo Ann said neither the sheriff nor any other officer ever spoke with her. The district attorney only asked her about the murder in the courtroom.

Prosecutors asked her specific questions about the tall man, the mask, and the gloves. She recalled the black shoes because they stood out the most. Jo Ann remembered the accused man on trial sitting in one of the courtrooms smirking at her during the trial. Her aunt Ruth stood by her during most of her testimonies in the courtrooms.

Was life good for the girls in Vernon after their parents were so cruelly taken from them? They said it was during my time with them. They talked of having a pet armadillo and bunnies, as well as chickens, horses, pigs, and cows. They laughed at naming the animals, who later became their food.

However, during the time I spent with Jo Ann and Jane in 2010, when they were seventy-two and sixty-eight years old, I sensed that their life in Vernon was not as good as they had implied, and that they had no love lost for their aunt Ruth. At one point toward the end of this meeting, Sue showed Jo Ann photographs of the house in Vernon and asked if she wanted the photos. Jo Ann vehemently announced that she did not "want any photographs of the hell house."

Follow-up Meeting with Jo Ann

In January 2011, I drove to Oklahoma to visit Jo Ann at her modest, well-kept brick home. Our time together was tranquil and peaceful.

We looked through photo albums, and I scanned family photos to help tell Roy and Mae's story. The memorabilia she shared with me was in a simple, small wooden antique trunk in the garage. Other items were in two brown Avon delivery boxes. Pieces of her life were missing because of the lack of personal items from her parents.

In the trunk was her mom's wedding outfit, a pink Battenberg lace two-piece dress. Mae had been tiny, about a size zero by today's sizing standards. Jo Ann pulled out her white cotton baby dress and gingerly touched it, saying Mae had made it for her. A painting by Mae of a duck hung on a bedroom wall, along with an oval frame photo of Jo Ann and her mother.

Jo Ann told me she herself played piano and said she had been an expert shooter in school. Her cat, Sweetie Pie, was indifferent to my visit. After all this time, she still loved cats.

I asked her once again to retell the events of that fateful night for me since I honored her wish not to record her. She recounted the same story without faltering while tears welled up in her eyes. Then she repeated the "hell house" comment.

As I sat with Jo Ann, I could not help but think about the trauma both she and her sister had carried with them, silently, since childhood and the questions that lingered over them for almost seven decades: who killed their parents and why.

Jo Ann and Jane Hunt sitting in front of their Hunt grandparents
piano the day their parents were murdered.

Lubbock Avalanche—Journal Archives

Mae and Roy Hunt standing on their back porch
in Littlefield with Jo Ann.

Jo Ann Hunt Price

GALVESTON SEASIDE

In the same forty-eight-hours that the Hunt daughters rode in silence to Vernon, officers arrived at a beachfront hotel in Galveston, Texas. A Texas highway patrolman pounded loudly on a hotel room door. A tall, disheveled man with dark hair and a strapping body slowly opened the door, wearing only pajama bottoms. Looking at each other with cagey eyes, they exchanged casual greetings.

"Are you Jim Thomas?" asked the patrolman.

Pausing and slyly smiling, the man said, "No."

Not trusting the answer, the patrolman slowly recalled the information he had been given earlier about this guy. In an atypical request, the officer asked, "Can you please pull down your pajama bottoms?"

Without a moment's hesitation and with a snarky smile, the man complied, dropping the pajamas to the floor. The officer bent low enough and quickly noted the large surgical scar on the man's right leg and immediately put two and two together. Based on the description from a Texas Ranger back in Lubbock, Texas, this was the man he needed to detain.

The officer gave the suspect time to dress before handcuffing him and driving him to Houston, Texas. His demeanor was business-like throughout the entire trip. No one told him why he was taken into custody, except that he was a person of interest in a crime committed near Lubbock.

After overnight transport to the Lubbock County jail, the suspect is immediately questioned by Texas Rangers and the Lamb County Sheriff to determine his whereabouts over the previous seventy-two hours. After two hours of nonstop questioning, the suspect, Jim Thomas, begins laughing. He refused further interrogation and was placed in a holding cell.

The ties between the long car ride and this arrest soon start to make sense, like deciphering a secret war code. The connection started with one significant event that occurred sixty-two days earlier on a hot, dusty August day, at the trial of a Cameron, Texas, physician who was convicted of attempted murder of a Littlefield doctor. A seven-year sentence had been imposed on this doctor for his crime, and his wife was about to go on trial as an accomplice in her role in that attempted murder.

Time moved quickly after the Cameron doctor's conviction, and no one could see the foreboding shadows quickly building over Littlefield. Those shadows descended on a cold, nearly moonless October night in 1943. But this was not the first time the dark shadows came to Littlefield for a visit.

THE DRUNK

When those dark shadows descended in October 1943, it came to light that this was not Littlefield's first plunge into darkness. Seven years prior, the Lamb County sheriff had been murdered during a gun battle near the town's train depot.

During this 1937 murder case, limited forensics were used to convict the alleged murderer, who met his end sitting in Old Sparky, the legendary electric chair in Huntsville, Texas.

"Hell no, I won't drop the gun. I will kill both you damn laws!" The words rang in Lamb County Sheriff Franklin Loyd's ears right before three bullets struck his body and knocked him to the ground as he attempted to arrest the man for public drunkenness. Being shot by a drunk who had been hitting the bottle since nine that morning was the last thing Loyd expected on a calm Saturday evening on March 20, 1937.

The drunken man waving and shooting the gun was Leroy Kelley, a thirty-two-year-old Black man who had been living in Littlefield for four years and could neither read nor write.

The day's hours passed monotonously for the sheriff and his deputy, Sam Hutson, both unaware that trouble was brewing in The Flats, a Black community north of the Littlefield railroad tracks.

Even though Littlefield was not a true southern town, it did exhibit southern traditions in terms of segregation. Racial lines were drawn by those east-to-west railroad tracks that divided it.

Later that afternoon, three black men told Loyd and Hutson about another black man raising a ruckus with a gun and cursing at everyone. That evening, after making a humanitarian grocery delivery, the two officers drove toward the Littlefield Train Depot, where they spotted Kelley staggering by the gas station. "It was like he was zigzagging and walked like he had stumped his toe," remarked Hutson.

Loyd stopped the car, and both men quickly opened the doors and got out without Kelley noticing.

Loyd nodded to Hutson, "What is that, a drunk?"

Hutson laughed, replying, "It looks like a drunk."

Loyd reached into the car and turned off the engine and lights. Shutting the car door, he approached the staggering Kelley.

"Wait a minute," Loyd yelled out. "I want to talk to you." Kelley did not stop.

Loyd continued, "Wait a minute. What's the matter with you? I want to talk to you."

When Kelley did not stop, Loyd ran toward him. Kelley looked back at the two lawmen and started trotting faster. As Loyd neared Kelley, he reached out toward him and encountered four bursts of gunfire. Hutson, who had been leaning on the car and not paying attention, was startled and started running toward Kelley, tackled him, and grabbed his hand. Scuffling, Hutson yelled, "Leroy, drop that gun. Don't do that."

Kelley yelled back, "Hell no, I won't drop my gun. I will kill both you damn laws."

Kelley was able to get off another shot at Hutson's feet during the struggle, and Hutson lost his hold on Kelley. As Hutson bent at the waist and panted to catch his breath, he turned and noticed Loyd crumpled on the ground. Loyd's pistol lay in front of him. The deputy never carried a gun when he was on rounds with Loyd. Only Loyd did. Hutson ran back, grabbed Loyd's gun, and fired at Kelley, hitting him in the arm.

Loyd had no law enforcement experience when the county commissioners appointed him sheriff of Lamb County on June 11, 1935. A humble Amherst druggist, dry goods merchant, and Mason, Loyd replaced Sheriff Len Irvin, who was serving a two-year federal sentence for fraud. Loyd soon became a vigorous law enforcement officer and widely hated among the lawless crowd.

The Shooting

For a drunken man chaotically shooting his pistol on a dark night, Kelley did a lot of damage to Loyd. Julian Krueger, a Lubbock doctor, did his best to save the sheriff, but the internal damages caused by the bullets were extensive. Loyd could move his arms, but a bullet had severed his spinal column. Another bullet had gone behind and below his left ear and exited his skull. The third one lodged behind his eighth rib.

During surgery, Dr. Krueger removed the bullet that severed Loyd's spinal column. As minutes turned into hours, it became clear that Loyd would never awake from his surgery. The forty-eight-year-old sheriff died a little over twenty-four hours after being shot.

Loyd's whispered last wish showed his true character. "I want no violence. Tell them the Negro should be given a hearing. The law must be allowed to take its course." Even with vigorous talk of an uprising in the county, the residents remained peaceful.

Numerous condolences came to Loyd's family from all over Texas, including one from Mrs. Vesta Redwine and her son, Deputy Sheriff Norvell Redwine, of Tahoka, Texas. "We can sympathize deeply with the family of Mr. Loyd." An inmate at the Lynn County Courthouse had killed her husband and Sheriff Redwine's father, Deputy Felix Redwine, with five bullets on March 6, 1936. That murderer, Elmo Banks, was executed in Huntsville, Texas.

Kelley's Trial

Charges were filed against Kelley after Loyd's funeral, and the trial was quick. The small town wanted expeditious justice for its beloved sheriff. In a special convened term, the Lamb County Grand Jury returned a murder indictment against Kelley on April 5. A special venire of sixty jurors was selected on April 6, and a trial was set for April 8, with Judge Clarence Russell presiding. Kelley's two attorneys were appointed on the day of the trial. On April 10, the jury came back in less than an hour with a death verdict, the first death penalty by a Lamb County jury.

Justice was promptly served in 1937. Three days after the indictment and nineteen days after the shooting, the jury fixed the death penalty upon Kelley.

The swift trial included testimony from the three boys who first reported Kelley's drunkenness, as well as from Hutson and Dr. Kreuger. Dr. Kreuger explained the extent of Loyd's wounds in his courtroom testimony. He even presented the fatal bullet in a vial before introducing it as evidence against Kelley, which is noteworthy considering that seven years later, the bullet that killed Roy Hunt was never presented at trial.

The most engaging witness to take the stand was Kelley himself. Throughout his trial, Kelley had sat dejected and huddled, gazing disinterestedly at the floor and barely glancing up.

When testifying, Kelley said, "I don't remember shooting Mr. Loyd the sheriff.... I [sure] don't remember nothin' that was said, no, suh. I am telling the truth. I hope God will kill me if I ain't telling the truth...."

Court records show no motion of continuance and few objections by Kelley's attorneys. Following court procedures for a death verdict, Kelley's attorneys, Eula Andrew (Andy) Bills, and James Gowdy filed eleven bills motioning for a new trial. One bill stated that the court erred in permitting Hutson to testify to the jury and what the three witnesses had said to him about Kelley's actions and conduct. Kelley signed these documents with an X.

Kelley was remanded to jail, with his sentence suspended until the appeal court's decision. Under early Texas judicial law, a formal sentence could not be set in a murder conviction until the Court of Criminal Appeals upheld or overturned the lower court's conviction.

The Court of Criminal Appeals stated that while the testimony comprised a series of prior misdemeanors, all the testimony was admissible because it showed the accused's state of mind at the time of the shooting and showed why Loyd was attempting to arrest Kelley.

On February 10, 1938, Judge Russell pronounced Kelley's death sentence and set his execution date.

The Execution

Kelley's life ended less than a year after his drunken killing rampage. As Kelley stepped into the execution chamber, he was asked if he had anything to say. He mumbled, "I'm ready to go." On March 15, 1938, Leroy Kelley became the 150th man to die in the Texas prison system's legendary Old Sparky.

Kelley's was the first murder trial in Lamb County to go to the Appeals Court. It found that evidence was properly presented, down to the bullet causing Loyd's death. The jury was presented a full medical examination of Loyd's death, including X-rays. Kelley testified in his own defense and his court-appointed lawyers made a proper appeal. The destitute and uneducated Kelley was provided the fairest of trials he could have expected in 1937, even though his court-appointed attorneys had almost no time to prepare a defense.

Aftermath

Grace Loyd completed her husband's term as Lamb County sheriff, serving from 1937 to 1939. She was named sheriff based on the traditional Texas custom, where the wife was first offered the position after her husband, acting in his official capacity as sheriff, dies. Historically, this practice varied from county to county throughout Texas and was often carried out so that the surviving spouse could maintain the family income.

Loyd's murder was soon forgotten, along with Kelley's execution. The townspeople happily went about their lives, with their unlocked doors and children playing out on the streets away from parents' watchful eyes.

Nothing significant in this small community happened until news of World War II began circulating through radio broadcasts and newspaper headlines. The greatest tragedy befalling the town at that time was when military service personnel arrived on doorsteps with telegrams for surviving family members, delivering the words that their sons or husbands had been killed or were missing in action.

All this changed on a pleasant May night in 1942. The town awoke to the shocking news that one of their beloved doctors was almost killed on the outskirts of Littlefield in a farmer's field. People were even more astounded when the victim told law officers that his assailant was another physician. The investigation into the attempted murder would reunite some familiar names from the Loyd murder: Deputy Sam Hutson, Judge Clarence Russell, Eula Andrew (Andy) Bills, and Deputy Norvell Redwine. And it was a harbinger of even greater tragedy yet to come.

Franklin Loyd was sheriff
of Lamb County from June
1935 until his murder in
March, 1937.
Clovis News Journal

Grace Loyd served out the
term of her husband's office
from 1937 to 1939.
Clovis News Journal

MIDNIGHT MEETING

On a cooler than normal, balmy night on May 20, 1942, four young men were at McCormick's Service Station in Littlefield on the Lubbock Highway: Buster Weaver, Clint Fagan, Howard Farley, and Doyce Hutto. Howard and Buster entered the station before midnight and grabbed some sodas and candy. Clint and Doyce arrived minutes later.

Naturally, they noticed the small brunette talking on the telephone mounted to a post in the center of the station. When the woman finished her subdued conversation after three or four minutes, she hung up, turned around, looked squarely at Howard and Buster and said, "Thank you," and walked out the front station door. The boys could not take their eyes off this young, slender, and well-dressed woman sauntering into the dark toward a car similar to a 1941 Buick.

After the woman got into the car on the passenger side, the car took off towards Lubbock. The young men continued with their late-night ritual of checking on their cars, drinking Cokes, and shooting the shit. It was the next day when they learned that a Littlefield doctor had been attacked only two miles east of the station, near the Blessing Farm just outside of town.

Earlier the previous day, Dr. Roy Hunt had spent his time tending to numerous patients. The night was turning cooler and was full of energy as friends arrived at Roy and Mae's home for an evening of dinner and bridge.

Like a ghost from his past, Ruth Nichols Newton, wife of Dr. Billy Newton, called Roy four times that night. The phone first rang at 8:15 p.m. Mae did not recognize the voice when Ruth asked to speak to Roy and Mae called him to the phone. Ruth told Roy she was in trouble and wanted him to come to Lubbock. "It would be impossible for me to do this," he stated and hung up.

About 8:45 p.m., Ruth called again, and Roy again refused to go to Lubbock. Persistent, Ruth called back at 11:00 p.m. and told Roy she would drive to Littlefield. Sometime between 11:45 p.m. and midnight, she called Roy again from McCormick's Service Station.

The Roadside Meeting

After the final phone call, Roy, who could be compared to a young Montgomery Cliff, was a handsome man with dark hair and mesmerizing blue eyes, grabbed his car keys, and left the house never telling Mae why he was leaving at the late hour.

Roy left their home right after midnight and drove two miles east of Littlefield, where he saw a car parked alongside the road. Driving up cautiously, he parked in front of the car and turned off his headlights.

Roy raised his left arm to shield his eyes when the lights from the other car illuminated him. After the lights dimmed, Roy opened his car door, stepped out, and approached the driver's side of the other car, and leaned in the window, recognizing his ex-girlfriend, Ruth, whom he had dated in medical school.

"I have not seen you in a long time," Roy remarked.

Ruth responded, "You sure are a hard man to get a hold of." Gesturing with her right hand toward the empty passenger seat, she invited him into the car because she said she wanted to talk to him.

Ruth Nichols Newton

Ruth was born in the "Athens of the Panhandle," in Clarendon, Texas, on a hot June day in 1913. After graduating from Clarendon High

School in 1931, she went to south Texas and entered the Professional School of Nursing at Jefferson Davis Hospital in Houston, specializing in dietetics and later becoming head of the hospital's obstetrics ward. This striking, slender girl with light brown hair and blue eyes graduated in September 1934 and worked as a graduate nurse until her termination on April 15, 1935, after school officials found out about her secret marriage to Billy Newton. In those days, nurses were not allowed to be married while attending nursing school.

Ruth was more than a conventional nurse, and friends and colleagues described her as dependable, pleasant, efficient, responsible, and effective in her work. However, this same woman was characterized as having a dark side of being promiscuous with men, a heavy drinker, and venomous. Most people said she was a girl who lived a wild life and caused trouble.

Rumors circulated among the staff regarding the relationship between Ruth and Roy after she married Billy because he was the total opposite of Roy, who was known to be crabby, domineering, and arrogant.

The Shooting

With the car's lights illuminating his path, Roy walked around the front of the car toward the passenger door. When he turned toward the car door, he recognized Billy Newton's familiar voice yelling from behind the car. Standing up from the tall grass and weeds, gun in hand, Billy shouted, "Hands up. Don't you know this woman is married?"

Without further warning, Billy fired five times at Roy, with two of those bullets striking Roy's body.

Stunned, Roy staggered, grabbed at his stomach, and fell into the grassy weeds outside the glow of the car's headlights. The gunman walked to the driver's side door and ordered Ruth to give him a flashlight. "I want to see what I have done to Roy. I am going back around to see if the son of a bitch is dead."

Gathering his wits and strength, Roy raised up and ran off the highway edge through a wooden fence and into a field. He laid down between two crop furrows and burrowed as close to the ground as his body would allow, thwarting Billy's efforts of finding him.

When the gunman discovered Roy had run off into the field, instead of following the wounded man's possible path with that flashlight, he repeatedly cursed and stomped back toward the driver's side, pushing Ruth aside. Billy climbed into the car, slammed the door, put the car in reverse, and turned the wheels back toward the field.

He drove the car back and forth several times, flashing the car lights on the pasture before finally giving up his efforts to spot Roy and heading back toward Lubbock.

Lying in the plowed field for an unknown time, Roy finally rose and staggered back to his car and drove to his hospital near downtown Littlefield.

William R. Newton

William Rowland (Billy) Newton, Jr. was born in the tiny town of Buckholts, Texas, in May 1909. The town itself did not have telephone service until 1914. Billy's father was the notable William Newton, Sr., who built the first Milam County hospital and served as State Senator of the 13th Senatorial District in the late 1930s.

Graduating from Cameron's Yoe High School in June 1926, he entered the University of Texas at Austin and later went to the University of Texas Medical School in Galveston in October 1929. Records show that Billy arrived at Jefferson Davis Hospital in July 1933 and stayed until June 1934. He joined the U.S. Army Medical Corps as a First Lieutenant and provided medical support to troops in central Texas.

According to co-workers, working with Billy at the hospital was like working with the fictional characters Dr. Jekyll and Mr. Hyde. Billy's temperament turned at the drop of a hat, and he always pushed himself because he thrived on publicity. However, to a certain degree, a few people considered him a likable man.

Colleagues remarked more than once that Billy was arrogant, hair-brained, erratic, egotistical, high-strung, and overbearing. None of the doctors who worked with him liked him because they had to supervise him constantly. For example, during a simple medical procedure on a patient with an arm injury, Billy did not pay close enough attention to what he was doing and sewed a four-inch-long and one-inch-wide piece of glass into the man's arm. His reaction to this was one of indignation and yelling. It proved he was radical and domineeringly aggressive because he refused to admit this grievous error to his superiors.

Women, on the other hand, were attracted to Billy's deep, strong, soothing voice, even when only talking to him on the telephone. Rumors circulated that he was a drug addict and associated with the drug business; however, those speculations were never confirmed.

What is most remarkable about the timing of this shooting is that the Newton Memorial Hospital was chartered on May 11, 1942, and officially opened on October 17th of that same year. The new hospital was separate from the Newton Clinic and was built within the home of his dad, Dr. William Newton, Sr. by building additions around the home to create the hospital portion.

Back to the Shooting

An hour and forty-five minutes had elapsed from when Roy left his home to when he stumbled into the Littlefield Hospital emergency room, where on-call nurses scrambled to get Roy onto a gurney to stabilize him. As Roy lay critically wounded, his brother, Dr. Ewell Hunt, answered a 2:00 a.m. phone call and was apprised of Roy's condition. On the dark two-lane Littlefield highway from Lubbock, Ewell drove as quickly as he could to the hospital to help save his brother's life.

Roy was in critical condition. He had been shot through the chest by a pistol, and the bullet had come out near his right shoulder blade. The other bullet ripped through his stomach and exited just left of his backbone, lacerating his intestines.

Ewell, along with Lubbock doctor Otis "Babe" English, operated on Roy and administered blood transfusions. Following surgery, Ewell said his brother had a fair chance at recovery, "The danger of infection is always present, and it may be days before any encouraging signs may be shown."

Ewell noted from the recovered bullets that Roy had been shot with a light caliber pistol; however, the size of the bullets was never stated or seen again.

The Arrest

Before his surgery, Roy told Sheriff Hutson that his attackers were Billy and Ruth Newton. In a weakened state, Roy signed a complaint against the Newtons, and the sheriff made plans to arrest the couple. Several times during the day, Roy said, "I would like to talk to the man and learn what the motive was."

Hutson contacted the Milam County sheriff's office and talked to Sheriff Sara White. She assigned Deputy Carl Black to begin searching around Cameron for the Newtons—at their home, at the home of Billy's mother, at the hospital, and elsewhere. Finally, tips led Black to call the Sterling Life Building in Houston. Black left for Houston around noon on May 21 to bring the Newtons back to Cameron.

Returning at about 10 p.m., White and Black stayed at the Newtons' home with them until Hutson arrived the next day to arrest the couple on assault charges with the intent to murder.

On May 22, flanked by a heavy guard of Texas Rangers and county officers, the Newtons were arraigned less than sixty yards from the Littlefield Hospital in Samuel Farquhar's Littlefield Justice of the Peace office. As if dressed for Sunday church, Billy wore an immaculate blue business suit and Ruth a white silk jersey turban and dress. Both sat calmly during the ten-minute hearing, never raising their eyes in any direction. The couple waived an examining trial, and bonds were set at $15,000 for Billy and $10,000 for Ruth.

After paying their bonds, the couple left Littlefield about forty-five minutes later. With Billy's thriving medical practice and growing family in Cameron, everyone speculated why Roy identified the Newtons as attempting to kill him. The most interesting development revealed from the ten-minute hearing was that the two doctors and Ruth had known each other in the 1930s.

Aftermath of the Shooting

Roy never explained why he left the house that night after those phone calls and traveled two miles east of Littlefield to see Ruth. The police reports alluded to the fact that when Roy left the house, he was either expecting to see a highway wreck or to help Ruth with an unwed pregnant woman she was taking to New Mexico.

Roy was certainly not fully honest, even with his brother Ewell, who asked him repeatedly why Billy would want to shoot him. Roy offered no reason but did say that he had dated Ruth prior to her marriage to Billy, when she was a nurse in training at the Jefferson Davis Hospital. He even admitted they even had two or three dates after she secretly married Billy. But Roy claimed that in his associations with Ruth, he did nothing that would provoke cause for Billy to want to shoot him.

It took Roy almost two months to recover from his gunshot wounds. Mae and the girls visited him in the hospital almost daily.

After the shooting and Roy's recovery, he and Mae changed their habits, especially at home. Maybe it was because of what had happened or because Roy knew more than he was saying about that roadside meeting. Either way, the couple kept their bedroom doors open at night, despite the small size of the house and the lack of privacy. They also started leaving the bathroom light on at night.

Ruth Newton.

Swisher County Appeal File, Austin

The Lamb County Courthouse, where the Newton couple
were arraigned and posted bond.

Christena Stephens

THREE-RING CIRCUS

The Newtons

Roy's accusation against the Newtons focused the community's attention on the doctor. Billy had a reputation as a vicious drunk who had been compared to Dr. Jekyll and Mr. Hyde.

Billy and Ruth Newton started dating after Billy left Jefferson Davis Hospital in Houston and opened a medical practice in Cameron. Ruth remained in Houston for ten months. Billy visited her several times, and on many occasions, colleagues observed them arguing. Their marriage license was issued in Cameron on April 15, 1935, and they were secretly married on April 16, 1935, at a Houston pastor's home.

Newtons' Grand Jury at Lamb County

Three months after this shooting, the Lamb County grand jury convened in early August 1942 at Olton, Texas, to hear the attempted murder evidence. Nine witness statements—including Roy's and four from the young men who saw Ruth at a service station—gave the grand jurors enough evidence to indict the Newtons on separate charges of assault with intent to murder.

Harold LaFont, District Attorney for the Texas 64th Judicial District, prepared the grand jury indictments against the Newtons and delivered them to Judge Clarence Russell. Roy's brief testimony about the night of the shooting included a statement that he had not seen the Newtons in seven years.

Carl Black, the Cameron deputy sheriff, testified about tracking the Newtons in Houston after he could not find them in Cameron. Mary Lou Patella, a switchboard operator at the Sterling National Life Insurance Company in Houston, told jurors that Billy had said good morning to her from the banister above her desk between 9:30 and 10:00 a.m. on May 21. Dr. Woodrow Avent, who worked for Billy, recalled seeing Billy on the afternoon of May 19 but not on May 20.

The four young men testified that they had seen Ruth using the phone at McCormick's Service Station around midnight, and that she thanked them after she hung up the phone and walked toward a Buick-like car.

No physical evidence was introduced to the grand jurors, not even the bullets recovered from Roy's body. The grand jury based their indictment on witness testimonies alone.

Attempting to Try the Newtons

From the Newtons' initial arrest in May 1942 to their first scheduled trial, bringing them to justice became a three-ring circus, starting with a doctor's note that delayed the first trial.

On August 31, 1942, a doctor's note arrived at the Lamb County Courthouse in Olton by Western Union telegram from the Hilton Hotel in Plainview. The note, dated August 30, 1942, was written on a prescription pad and addressed to the Lamb County District Judge:

> This is to certify I have seen Dr. and Mrs. Billy Newton, Jr. on 8/29 and 8/30/42 and find them suffering with ptomaine poisoning. It is my opinion they will be incapacitated and physically unable to attend court for several days. Signed, H.W. Poetter, M.D. (Henry Poetter).

It was entered into court as Exhibit A, and the Newton case was postponed. Dr. Poetter was a doctor and partner in the Newton Memorial Hospital.

Seven months later, their case was rescheduled again after both the state and defense attorneys indicated that they would not be ready to try the Newtons on March 8, 1943. They were unable to subpoena the four young men as witnesses because they were now in the Armed Forces. The attorneys said the servicemen were trying to obtain furloughs so that they could testify.

Judge Clarence Russell, the 64th District Judge, known for his stoic nature, allowed the attorneys time to determine the witnesses' availability because most were serving in the Army.

The third postponement came two months later because a member of the defense counsel was engaged in legislative duties in Austin, leaving spectators walking away from the courthouse still not knowing anything related to this case or the motive behind the alleged shooting.

Finally, on August 23, 1943, Billy's trial began—fifteen months after the alleged shooting.

Andy Bills, a Littlefield attorney assigned to the Newtons' prosecution cases, repeatedly encouraged Harold LaFont, the district attorney, to talk to Roy and the other witnesses before the trial. LaFont ignored the advice, finally speaking to Roy the day before the trial. LaFont never spoke to the other witnesses.

Billy's First Trial

The circus of trial postponements finally ended on a sweltering Monday morning in August 1943 in Judge Russell's courtroom. Billy's trial might have seemed insignificant as World War II raged across Europe and in the Pacific, but in Lamb County, it dominated the headlines and was on everyone's mind.

As the trial began, the small second-floor courtroom in Olton was standing room only, with observers packed in wall-to-wall. The windows were raised, but only the slightest breeze circulated. Billy appeared relaxed. Only the twitching fingers in his lap signaled his agitation. He often stroked either his chin or face during the first day of trial.

Ruth appeared in court for the start of the trial, but after Judge Russell separated her case from her husband's—her trial would begin after his—she left shortly after the ruling, reportedly to stay with her parents in Clarendon.

Harold LaFont and Andy Bills were the attorneys for the State. Jury selection started at 1:30 p.m. and was completed three hours later. Thirty-six subpoenas were issued for the trial.

The Defense called thirty-eight witnesses, who each testified that Billy was in Cameron and Houston on May 21, 1942. Twenty of those witnesses claimed they saw him in and around Cameron as late as 7:00 p.m.

Prosecutors presented twelve witnesses who tied the Newtons to the assault. Roy, the state's primary witness, took the stand and testified that the Newtons were at the shooting scene when he was attacked.

Wearing a light tan, tropical worsted suit with a white shirt and tan tie, Roy gave his testimony in a calm, confident manner while maintaining that he did not know the cause of the shooting. He often sat in the courtroom by himself, rarely conversing with the prosecutors, a mix of emotions crossing his handsome face.

The state relied chiefly on Roy's testimony and didn't introduce any physical evidence—not even the two bullets extracted from Roy's body.

In the musty courtroom, spectators sticky with perspiration laid down their paper fans when Roy took the stand. For two days, he testified about the night he was shot.

"Dr. Newton shot me and Mrs. Newton, his wife, was present at the time," he said. "The shooting took place about two miles east of Littlefield, on the Lubbock Highway." He would later testify that he had left his house after receiving three phone calls earlier in the evening from Ruth. However, he never said what the calls were about or why he agreed to meet them on the highway late at night.

Roy went on to discuss his relationship with Billy and Ruth:

I first knew Dr. Newton, the defendant in this case, at Galveston Medical School. I first met Dr. Newton in the fall of 1930 when I went to school down there. He was a student at the university there. I saw him practically every day. Sure, I have had conversations with him during the time I was in school there, lots of times. We all called him "Billy" in school.

Dr. Newton and I were in school together either two or three years; He left school first. I left Galveston in 1934, July. I went to the same hospital, Jefferson Davis. As to whether I knew Dr. Billy Newton there, he left the year I came; his internship was up when I entered. I knew Dr. Newton's wife there in Houston; I knew her well. She was a graduate nurse at the institution. I had occasion to be around her there at the hospital; I was around her practically every day for the length of time she was there, which was about eight months after I came there. She went by the name of Nichols.

I went with her there while I was an intern; I was with her quite often. The last time I saw Mrs. Newton prior to the time I was shot here at Littlefield, was, I imagine, about two months after she left the hospital. She came back down there on a visit probably three months after she left the hospital in 1935.... I first knew she was the wife of Dr. Newton when she quit her job and packed up—the night she left Jefferson Davis Hospital. I asked her why she was leaving and she said she was married.

Roy said he hadn't seen Ruth again until the night of the shooting. That night, shortly after midnight, he said he went to meet Ruth on the highway, and when he arrived, he saw a car with its lights on parked on the right side of the road. Roy stopped, walked up to the car, and saw Ruth sitting behind the wheel.

I...walked up to the car and leaned on it and saw Mrs. Nichols. I said, "Ruth it has been a long time since I have seen you." She was sitting right in the car under the steering wheel and I was looking her in the face. She said "You're a hard man to get hold of. Come on the other side and get in; I want to talk to you. It will take just two minutes."

And so I walked around on the other side, and, when I got nearly to the car, nearly to the front door on the other side, I heard some noise back there behind the car at the burrow pit. I looked around and there was somebody walking up there and I saw it was a man. When he got up to the rear of the car, almost to the rear of the car, he says, "Hands up. Don't you know this woman is married?"

And he stepped into the light of the parking lights and pulled his gun up and shot me twice. That is all there was to it. I didn't have time to dodge, get my hands up or do anything, except just fall. He shot me twice. He walked around on the other side of the car and says to Mrs. Newton, "Give me the flashlight and let's see what I have done."

Roy said he recognized Billy Newton's voice as he spoke, and as he stepped into the light, he could see Billy's face. Roy went on:

I found out I could get up, and I got up to run off. When he heard me get up, he was on the other side of the car, and when he saw me running off he hollered, "Halt." I wasn't about to halt; I wasn't going to stop.

At any rate, I fell down instead of halting. I fell over behind the slope of the borrow pit. He shot at me just as I fell but didn't hit me. I ran on down the borrow pit probably seventy-five feet and crawled over a fence and ran out into the field there and laid down between some furrows. I couldn't tell whether he got in the car or not, but somebody in the car, either he or Mrs. Newton, turned the lights around and shined them out over there, and as they did I laid down between these ridges and the lights would go over me and they couldn't see me.

Then they got in the car and drove up toward Mr. Blessing's about a quarter of a mile, and again turned around and threw their lights all over the territory there and then drove back down to where he first shot me and threw their lights out there again, but couldn't come out after me, and pretty soon they drove off toward Lubbock.

I just laid there for about ten minutes. . .until I was sure they weren't coming back—or felt like they weren't—and then I went back to my car. I crawled up the side of the road—it was fairly dark. I got in [my car] and drove it back to Littlefield. I went to the Littlefield Hospital and stopped the car and got out and walked in the hospital. From there I took my clothes off with the help of the nurse. I took a quarter grain of morphine, a thousand c.c.'s of glucose, some lock jaw serum, tetanus anti-toxin, and gave orders.

I knew I was seriously wounded, I could tell where I was shot. This arm was completely paralyzed; I had no use of it at all. And I knew I was shot through the stomach, of course. In the majority of cases bullet wounds in the stomach are fatal. I recognized my condition....

I was operated on to remove the bullets. Dr. English and my brother, Dr. Hunt, at Lubbock performed the operation. The operation was performed probably about two hours after I got back to the hospital; I got back about 12:30 and the operation was performed about 3:00. It was the first operation and I was operated on again ten days later.

Under cross examination by Emory Camp, Roy insisted that he and Billy had been good friends and had no hard feelings between them.

"I know of no reason at all why Dr. Billy Newton should have wanted to drive out here and shoot me except I used to go with Mrs. Newton," he commented. "It was seven years ago."

In Billy's defense, Carl Black, the deputy sheriff, testified that he could not locate the Newtons in Cameron and that he later arrested them in Houston at about 3:00 p.m. Another twenty-three witnesses testified to Billy's character, indicating that he was a peaceable and law-abiding citizen. Eleven witnesses said they saw him in Cameron, Houston, or places in between.

The courtroom went still as Billy, wearing a white suit with a bow tie and white shoes, took his seat in the witness chair. He began testifying in his own defense. His Mr. Hyde personality came through with a crook of a smile while raising his right hand and swearing on the Bible, "I swear to tell the truth, the whole truth and nothing but the truth." He claimed he was not near Littlefield on the night of May 21, and went on to describe his days from May 18 to May 20 in meticulous detail, including giving a patient ten units of estrogenic hormones and how much gas Ruth put in one of his cars. Most of his testimony recapped his personal life, even ensuring the jury knew his oldest child was seven.

He said that he and Ruth went to Houston on the evening of May 20. On the way, they stopped at about sundown in Caldwell at a filling station, where they ran into Sheriff Clint Lewis and shared soft drinks with him. At about 10:30 p.m., Billy and Ruth arrived at the Sterling National Life Insurance Company in Houston. After they arrived, they met their friend Bert Weathered. The next morning, the Newtons visited Houston police officer B.L. Ingram at his home. Eating breakfast at Ones-a-Meal, they returned to the insurance building, where Billy called Dr. Woodrow Avent around 11:00 a.m.

Billy claimed he had never been near Littlefield, except when he was chopping cotton near Lubbock when he was about twelve years old. He was adamant in his denial about shooting Roy: "I was where I said I was, and I did not shoot and couldn't have shot Dr. Hunt. It would have been impossible."

D.A. LaFont's cross-examination of Billy had little to do with the actual shooting. He asked about Billy's anatomy classes in medical school and his medical time in Houston. LaFont never asked about the relationship between Billy and Roy or anything about what happened the day before the shooting.

The jury took a little more than an hour to find Billy guilty on the evening of August 26, sentencing him to seven years in prison. Billy was silent and emotionless after the verdict, in contrast to his Jekyll-and-Hyde reputation.

After the trial, witnesses milled around on the street corners in Olton, a few in shocked disbelief because it had taken so long to bring this case to trial. They even voiced that one nagging unanswered question on everyone's mind: What was the motive for the shooting?

Jurors did not heed the character testimonies nor Billy's alibi. He had tried to argue he was in a different place. The alibis provided by the trial witnesses became a central argument in his motion for a new trial while he was still sitting in a Littlefield jail cell, but the motion was overruled. He entered into a $10,000 recognizance bond following the verdict to appeal to the state court.

Roy, who showed no emotion and little interaction throughout the trial, left the courthouse alone and without talking to anyone, as though the matter was over. Getting back into his car, he drove off steadily into the approaching night.

Trying Ruth

Billy was convicted on the same day Ruth's trial was scheduled to begin in Lamb County. The proceedings followed the same procedures as her husband's, with most of the same witnesses. As the court was about to convene that morning, a handwritten letter on Hilton Hotel letterhead signed by a Dr. Don Jones of Plainview certified that he had examined Ruth and that she was in a nervous prostrated condition and menstruating. He recommended that she rest in bed for about ten days.

Once again, this thirty-three-year-old woman was deemed too physically ill and unable to appear for her trial. Lawyers also cited that two Houston witnesses were unavailable to testify in her defense.

A second motion of continuance was filed for Ruth's case, with the court granting the application.

The Lamb County Courthouse in Olton, Texas.
Texas Department of Transportation

LIFE AMONGST COTTONFIELDS

Looking at Roy Hunt's and Mae Franks Hunt's portraits, it is easy to imagine them being high school sweethearts raised in a Texas town. The couple's courtship was far from such an idealistic scenario for the 1940s, but their life after they married seemed like a perfectionistic young romance story.

The couple met at Jefferson Davis Hospital sometime in 1936 or early 1937. They married in May 1937, on Mother's Day, with Mae's mother serving as matron of honor.

The limited family history provides enough details to give an indication of their characters and personalities as a loving couple intent on making a long-term home in Littlefield.

The Hunt Family

Roy's family was among the first to settle in the Lubbock area in the 1880s. George Maddon Hunt, the family patriarch, hailed from Clinton

County, Ohio, and was a farmer, hog buyer, teacher, and poet. Friends admired the Irishman for his integrity, fair dealing, and gentleman's heart. He seemed to have a natural gift for literacy in both writing and reading.

George and his first wife, Lydia Ann Wildman, had two children, Evie and Homer. Lydia died when Homer was only three weeks old, possibly from complications during childbirth. George later married Lina Taylor on New Year's Eve 1868, and their family grew to include Irvin, Sylva, Myrtle, Lottie, Alvin, and Clifford. Because Lina suffered from poor health, George moved his family to Denver, Colorado, in 1882 and later to Sterling, Kansas, in August 1883, probably following the Quaker settlements in which Lina's mother was a prominent minister.

In November 1884, the family moved to Texas in a horse-drawn wagon, but not before George cast his vote in the presidential election between James Blaine and Grover Cleveland. (Who he voted for is unknown.)

In his book, *Early Days Upon The Plains of Texas*, published in 1919, George recalled entering the Texas Panhandle, which he described as a treeless landscape with crystal-clear waters and abundant wildlife that included turkey, deer, wild horses, and wild hogs. Pronghorn antelope numbered in the thousands.

The Panhandle's mother town, Mobeetie, was the first they came to after leaving Dodge City, Kansas. George showed off his pet horse, Jimmie, to the locals by saying, "If I should step in front of him and say, 'howdy,' he would lift his leg for a shake."

The family left Mobeetie and traveled south, stopping at the Quitaque Ranch near Tule Canyon, where the children met a pet black bear. After leaving Quitaque, they lost their way and came across a group of cowboys at C.C. Slaughter's Circle Ranch in Hale County.

After the cowboys gave the Hunts correct directions, they invited the family to share a dinner of range food: prairie dogs. Prairie dogs were abundant in the region, numbering in the hundreds of thousands. George and his family gratefully accepted and ate the rodents for the first and last time.

By December 1884, the family arrived at the Quaker Colony of Estacado in Crosby County. Soon after, other settlers began moving away from this tiny community, and George moved the family to the new-formed town of Lubbock in 1890, where he became an early settler and pioneer. He wore the hats of the Justice of the Peace, grocery store owner, and manager of the Nicolett Hotel, all the while raising his family.

Roy Hunt

In January 1907, George's grandson, Roy, was born to his son, Alvin, and daughter-in-law, Lillie May. Roy's family included three brothers, Ewell, Homer, and A.B.; one sister, Ruth; and a stepbrother, June Cannon. Roy's father ran a grocery business for thirty-three years in Lubbock.

Life was not easy for the Alvin Hunt family. They experienced two significant tragedies. Their home burned down on January 1, 1913. The fire started early that morning, forcing the family to run out of the house in their bedclothes. The only possession they saved was a laundry sack that six-year-old Roy had stumbled over and grabbed off the front porch as he fled the burning house.

In March 1921, eight years after the Hunts lost their home, Lillie became ill with influenza. At that time, no antibiotics were available, so family members rubbed camphorated oil on her chest and administered aspirin in hopes of lowering her fever. Lillie died after her lungs filled with fluid, causing pulmonary edema. As one last act of love before she died, she gathered strength and baked her husband a birthday cake.

Roy graduated from Lubbock High School in 1924, where he served as class president and a halfback on the football team. He started college at the University of Texas and transferred to Texas Technological College in 1930 to fulfill the pre-medical requirements. He later entered the UT medical school at Galveston in October 1930, becoming a member of the Nu Sigma Nu fraternity.

After graduating on May 31, 1934, Roy transferred to Jefferson Davis Hospital in Houston to complete his internship. He worked as a junior and senior intern, as well as a chief resident specializing in surgery until May 1937.

Family, friends, colleagues, even hospital maids, characterized Roy as a fine man and student. He was quiet, efficient, and reserved. Like many young doctors, Roy dated nurses, but he had a reputation for being a gentleman and never discussed his personal life.

Toward the end of his residency, Roy started thinking of his future. In April 1937, he met with Dr. Thomas Duke in Littlefield, and they formed a partnership to establish a new Littlefield Hospital. Roy came on board as a surgeon, specializing in urology and women's health. They set up offices above Sadler's Drug Store on Main Street until the new hospital was completed on November 1, 1938. The new facility was a one-story, state-of-the-art, white brick building with a sizeable round, brick pond in front stocked with koi.

What the Doctor Built

To get a sense of what these doctors envisioned for this small community, I toured the original Littlefield Hospital in February 2011 with my friend Ginny Phillips and Sue Sexton, Roy Hunt's niece.

The hospital had been abandoned since the early 1980s and was severely rundown. We entered the building through the emergency room doors in the back of the building and were struck by a cold, dank, musky smell. It was also dark. The facility had no electricity, forcing us to use flashlights to illuminate our tour. Owls and pigeons were the only living inhabitants.

Ceiling tiles and insulation had fallen to the floor in various sections, and vandals had contributed to the destruction; however, most of the deterioration came from time and water damage.

Long hallways connected the entire facility to the medical rooms, patient rooms, and doctors' offices. On the second floor, natural light flooded in, and opportunistic pigeons flew from their makeshift perches. The different colors of stucco indicated that this was a more recent addition than the first floor. The facility had about fifty patient rooms. Only a few medical records remained in the newer second-floor addition. I had hoped to find old medical records that the doctors left in the basement.

The ceiling on the first floor had been lowered for a fire suppression sprinkler system. Our flashlights lit up the now open ceiling, revealing the wooden ceiling and white bricks of the building's oldest section.

The original hospital was at the center of the entire structure, with two wings and an upper level built around it, and included only four exam rooms, an X-ray room, laboratory rooms, an emergency bay, and a main surgical room. A nursery sat right in the middle of the hospital, with sizeable bay windows on two sides.

A long hallway going west connected ten patient rooms, file rooms, and doctors' offices. The windows in this section had been bricked up at some point, causing us to speculate as to why.

A faded flower mural had rapidly decayed in the main foyer of the hospital. East of the mural was another long section of doctors' offices and exam rooms covered in dark curved paneling and more bricked-up windows.

The visit gave me a better sense of what Roy and Dr. Thomas Duke had built for Littlefield's first formal hospital to treat and care for the community. The hospital had been a grand facility for its time but was now home to only ghosts and the beating wings of pigeons.

Mae Franks Hunt

In August 1917, Mattie Mae Franks was born in Galveston to Mattie and Charles Franks, a real estate agent. Mae was raised in a large family of three sisters and six brothers—who all survived the horrors of World War II.

During her high school years, Mae participated in many activities, including tennis and the Girl's Glee Club, and she was a leader in physical education and the drum corps. She graduated from John H. Reagan High School in Houston in August 1935, and her yearbook was filled with signatures and written notes for best wishes from friends. She entered the Jefferson Davis Hospital nurse's training program a month later, on September 15, 1935, and resigned on May 1, 1937, never graduating. Mae's daughter, Jo Ann, described her mother as a creative artist who adored painting and enjoyed playing cards. Mae also did embroidery and crochet and made Halloween costumes for her daughters and other kids. Unfortunately, no other information exists on Mae's early years.

The Hunts' Life

After Roy and Mae briefly visited Littlefield in May 1937, they acquired their marriage license in Lubbock and were married in Houston. The couple moved to the small rural town, which was a huge adjustment for Mae, who had only lived in Galveston and Houston. Moving into the Cooper Apartments, the Hunts' married life began in a community surrounded by cotton fields. Roy's relatives visited the couple a month after they arrived, welcoming Mae into the family along with a variety of gifts.

Soon, the Littlefield Rotary Club recruited Roy, where he served on the board of directors and various committees, including the Aims and Objects Committee, Fellowship Committee, and Health Committee.

The couple welcomed their first daughter, Jo Ann, in January 1938, with Roy's brother Ewell as the attending physician. A second daughter, Jane, was born nearly four years later.

Sometime before the 1940 Census, the Hunts moved into a small $2,500 brick home. Roy's modest annual income from various sources was $50, but he reported no monetary salary for the fifty weeks he worked in 1939, even though he typically worked about eighty-five hours a week.

Life for the Hunt family was conventional for that era. They traveled frequently to New Mexico, and the Littlefield newspaper society column regularly said the trips were "for business." The couple spent most of their time in Red River, New Mexico, while their daughters stayed with Roy's parents or the Dukes.

Roy had been known as an exceptional surgeon at Jefferson Davis Hospital, but in Littlefield, his days were mostly filled with routine tonsillectomies, colds, and basic operations. However, he performed one extraordinary surgery on eighteen-month-old Jim Brown.

Jim's father, Gaston Brown, owned and operated the Amherst Bakery in a small-town west of Littlefield. One evening, while Gaston was baking bread for the next day, Jim's mother, Ruby, stopped by the bakery and sat Jim down on the floor. The boy stood up and wandered off behind a dough mixer. Curiosity took hold, and he reached through the opening in the machine with his right hand while the gears were turning the mixing drum. The gears caught his hand and started to pull it through. Jim screamed as the motor began to strain against his hand. Gaston raced over and cut the power, causing the gears to back up, releasing Jim's hand.

The gears crushed the boy's pinky and ring fingers and severely injured his other two, although they remained intact. Seeing their son's crushed hand, the shocked parents rushed him along the dirt road to the Littlefield Hospital, where Roy worked for hours to salvage what remained of the boy's hand. While the actual date of the incident is unknown, the accident probably occurred between 1939 and 1941.

Roy attended to many patients that he considered friends and unfortunately later served as a pallbearer at many of his patients' funerals. For a short while, his brother, A.B., was the hospital's bill collector, and he would travel around the county requesting payments from patients. When the farmers could not pay with cash, they would often give A.B. a cow, chickens or other livestock. A.B. would sell them and deposit the funds in the hospital's bank account.

The Hunts' social life was emblematic of rural West Texas, with Roy enticing Mae into playing bridge with other couples at least two or three times every week. Even when the Hunts dined out with friends, the party moved back to their home afterward to play bridge.

Mae attended many bridal showers, going-away parties, birthdays, bridge games, housewarming functions, and soldier send-offs. When she could not attend, she would send gifts.

By 1943, the curly-haired Jo Ann was already acting as a socialite, carrying on with ladylike mannerisms and helping her mother give parties, especially farewell parties for the nurses at her dad's hospital. Jo Ann would present the gifts to attendees, often with a small curtsy.

Lamb County and Littlefield

Imagine arriving to a flat landscape in a horse-drawn buggy in 1876. The emptiness sweeps on for miles, with no trees and only a few rudimentary buildings or homes in sight.

What grass does manage to grow is barely green, adding to the sense of desolation. The only thing making this stark landscape even worth staying for is the stunning sunsets painting the western skies with colors of yellow, blue, orange, and red.

That's what the early settlers of Littlefield lived with for a few years. Then, brick buildings sprung up in town, hiding the flatness from immediate view. To brighten their homes, residents planted trees, flowers, and gardens. Rows of cotton turned the barren landscape into a sea of green and then white for a few months out of the year. Gradually, the landscape changed. Only the sunsets and sunrises being a constant. That was Littlefield, Texas.

As is common with all frontier and early settlements, comedy, tragedy, romance, and mystery mingled with the local history. The earliest settlers were first- or second-generation Germans who came either by covered wagon or train. Voters organized Lamb County in 1908 and naming Olton as the county seat. The sparsely populated area didn't have enough people to sign the petition for incorporation, so residents added the names of every local horse and mule, and cowboys even signed their sweetheart's names.

The first courthouse was built in 1908, and the wooden structure later caught fire and burned. A second courthouse was constructed in 1921.

The main distractions on the lonesome prairie in those early days were the hunting of coyotes, which settlers considered pests, and pronghorn antelope and jackrabbits, which they hunted for food. Canned peaches were more valuable than gold. Before the trains, the settlers received their mail by mules and their food by wagons from Lubbock.

In 1901, Austin banker and rancher George W. Littlefield had acquired more than 300,000 acres of the XIT Ranch, most of which was in Lamb County. In 1912, after learning that the Santa Fe railroad planned to build a cutoff line connecting its central Texas lines to its New Mexico route, Littlefield decided to begin colonizing his lands and laid out the townsite that bears his name.

Soon passenger express trains with observation, diner, and lounge cars, brought quick, safe, and luxurious travel through Lamb County on the way to New Mexico. In addition, ranchers began shipping cattle by train rather than driving them to market with cowboys and horses.

As the community grew, so did the need for medical care. Dr. Jeff Davis arrived on horseback in the spring of 1913. Most early doctors in rural areas saw patients in their homes, which meant traveling by horse or buggy at night over cattle trails—often through snow, ice, wind, or rainstorms. In 1915, Dr. O.B. Lynch came to Littlefield and left a year later, concluding that his doctoring services were not needed. In 1917, Dr. W.H. Anderson arrived with his daughter, Dorothy, and her dog, Vickie. As the story goes, Vickie apparently yipped and barked at every telegraph pole they passed from Fort Worth to Littlefield. Vickie's barking announced their arrival in Littlefield. When the 1923 flu epidemic hit, Anderson put himself to bed for three weeks as an example of how both flu patients and healthy residents should care for themselves. Dr. Anderson served Littlefield until 1931.

Littlefield's population reached two hundred fifty in 1915, and two years later, the first edition of the *Lamb County News* was published. The first commercial site was a grocery store, followed by the McAdams Lumber Company, a barbershop, a library, and a confectionery. Sadler's Drug Store soon followed, along with the Littlefield State Bank. Eventually, the surrounding ranchland was converted into agricultural crops, first with the help of mules and then tractors in the late 1920s.

By 1924, Littlefield was incorporated, with the population increasing to three thousand five hundred by 1930. Farmers produced cotton, sorghum, and a variety of vegetables. Over time, grain elevators, gins, a compress, and cottonseed oil mills competed with the frequent winds for noise.

Littlefield's first hotel later became the Payne-Shotwell Hospital in May 1937.

Littlefield was a quintessential small town, in which people all knew each other by their first names and the story of a young boy getting a black and white collie pup made front-page news. Doors stayed unlocked, and children roamed freely without fear.

By 1940, the population topped three thousand eight hundred. World War II began to affect the small community through gas and food rationing and the cancellation of the 1942 high school football season.

Other than Sheriff Loyd's murder in 1937 and the Klan march in 1924, life in Littlefield was humdrum until Roy's attempted murder in 1942. Rumors spread like a prairie fire about that entire incident, but even after Billy Newton's trial, the residents were left to speculate about a motive for the shooting.

The fall of 1943 was one of the driest on record for much of Texas. In Littlefield, the grass had been brown for months. Leaves fell and drifted with the ever-present winds.

Then, in October, sixty-two days after Billy Newton's conviction, the silent streets of Littlefield changed horrifically.

Downtown Littlefield, 1930.
Christena Stephens

Mae Hunt.
Jo Ann Hunt Price

Roy and Mae Hunt in
the snow behind the
nursery at their home.
Jo Ann Hunt Price

Roy and Jo Ann Hunt.
Jo Ann Hunt Price

Roy Hunt at his office desk at Littlefield Hospital.

Jo Ann Hunt Price

Mae and Roy Hunt.

Jo Ann Hunt Price

The Littlefield Hospital Clinic front entrance as it looks today.
Christena Stephens

7

MURDERER IN
THE SHADOWS

Hours Before the Murders

On October 25, 1943, Roy had a busy day tending patients at his clinic and out in the county. He returned late to Littlefield after being out with Dr. Fred Janes making house calls.

Roy's home was a harbor after long days of seeing patients and performing surgeries. It was a place for their friends and family to gather for meals, visits, and card games.

On this October night, the Hunt couple played poker with Janes and his wife Opal, as well as Roy Granbery, who was an abstractor for Lamb County. According to Fred, Mae cooked everyone dinner, and the evening was spirited.

When the Hunts waved goodbye to their guests from their small alcove front porch at about 2:20 a.m. on October 26, 1943, it was the last time they were seen alive. Retiring to their bed and saying goodnight with a kiss and with thoughts of the next day, the couple soon fell asleep.

Unknown to anyone, a murderer hid in the dark shadows of the Littlefield streets during those early morning hours as the couple turned out the last light.

The Hunts' tiny five-room brick home was located four blocks southeast of downtown Littlefield. A four-and-a-half-foot paling fence surrounded the backyard, except for a three-foot section connected to the east side at the back of the house. A four-foot hedge was on the east side, outside the fence. On the same block, three houses were to the west of the Hunt home, and three were to the east.

A chilly north wind blew, swaying the streetlights and causing their amber glow to shimmer in the pre-dawn darkness. A crispness and fog greeted workers as the cotton gins rumbled to life. Most other townsfolk still slept. Streets were eerily quiet, not even house sparrows, American robins, or blue jays were rousing from their slumber yet.

Littlefield's residents began their day with coffee and breakfast before sending their kids off to school or going to work. Most people were either listening to the radio or reading the newspaper to learn the latest updates on World War II.

Right before 8:00 a.m., Littlefield changed from a secure, quintessential town to a place of headline murders.

The Discovery

Mayda Grissom pulled her coat a little tighter as she left her house and walked to her car on that windy, cold morning. With the early morning fog lifting as dawn broke, she caught sight of two little girls running toward her in their bedclothes and coats. Mayda bent down as they approached. The oldest girl's cries were hard for her to understand, but Mayda soon grasped through Jo Ann's words that something horrible had occurred in the Hunt home three houses down.

Gathering the girls, Mayda took them into her home as her husband, Lou Grissom, waited outside their front door. Jo Ann kept crying. She refused to go back to her home with the couple. The Grissoms left her in their house and walked down to the Hunt home, with Mayda carrying Jane.

Lou Grissom, a wholesale oil dealer for Gulf Wholesale Oil, entered first. It was just before 8:00 a.m. He knocked on the front door and repeatedly called out but received no response. His hand reached for the doorknob. It was unlocked. He pushed open the front door. The house was encased in partial darkness. His gut knew something was seriously wrong in the house. He paused to let his eyes adjust, still calling out to Roy and Mae, before walking two steps into the front bedroom. Lou immediately whiffed the unpleasant odor.

Mayda had followed behind Lou with Jane. She walked towards the nursery in the southeast corner of the house. As she entered the room, she noticed that Jane's bed had a protective net to guard against insects, and the south nursery window was wide open.

Mayda turned and walked back towards the living room and joined her husband in the Hunts' bedroom. In the dark north corner of the room, Mayda saw Roy on the bed, his head covered in blood. Lou, standing on the right side of the bed, discovered Mae. Her face was shielded by the grotesque position of Roy's bound arms, which were tied to hers.

Both Lou and Mayda stood speechless and paralyzed as they looked at the bodies. When Lou regained his faculties, he turned and stepped into the living room to use the Hunt telephone. He called the Littlefield Hospital first, telling Mrs. Ralph Lair, superintendent of nurses, to notify Janes. Then, Lou called the operator and asked her to call law enforcement.

With his siren piercing the quiet morning, Lamb County Sheriff Sam Hutson arrived ten minutes later, bringing his chief deputy, Sid Hopping. Before walking into the Hunt home, Mayda recounted to Hutson what Jo Ann had said to her in front of her house. Lou stood up from the couch, looking as white as a sheet, when Hutson and Hopping entered the front door. They silently nodded at each other. Hutson removed his hat as he stepped into the bedroom.

Finding the light switch, he breathed forcefully as he viewed the scene. "Good God! Is that what that little child saw? It is impossible," he bellowed. He walked up to the bedside, flinging the bedspread over the Hunts with one hand.

Janes, meanwhile, had left his home in Olton, racing at top speed toward Littlefield, twenty-seven miles away. He arrived, disheveled, around 9:00 a.m.

Using the Hunt telephone, Hutson called Aubrey Fawver, the Lubbock Police Department Identification Officer/Investigator, who arrived at about 9:20 a.m. Fawver brought local Texas Rangers Norvell Redwine and Levi Duncan with him. After his father's murder in Lynn County, Redwine joined the Rangers in 1941. Deputy Sheriff Parum Posey also arrived, and later, the officers called Harold LaFont, the district attorney, to the scene.

They contacted Ed Watson with the *Lubbock Avalanche-Journal* to take crime scene photos.

Then, they called Roy's brother, Ewell, who made the thirty-six-mile drive from Lubbock, his mind no doubt racked with grief and asking a multitude of questions. Why, God, why? Who had done this? How were his nieces? When he got to the house, he confronted a horrific scene.

The Crime Scene

The Hunts' bodies lay in their double bed in the northeast corner of the house. Blood splatter covered almost everything in the bedroom. Rugs, strewn on the floor, were shredded. The small closet door was open, and clothes hangers lay scattered on the floor.

A lamp cord from the bedside table had been cut in two places, near the plug and the lamp base. At the head of the bed were two broken blinds and a cracked windowpane.

The bed was two feet from the north wall with its head to the east. The upper section of the mattress and sheets were soaked in blood and the bodies were brutalized.

Roy was on the left side; Mae to his right, their heads toward the east. Roy had clearly been shot, and his jaw was bashed in. Mae had been bludgeoned. The couple's hands and feet were tied together with a wire clothes hanger and a necktie around each of their necks. Mae had a handkerchief lying across her mouth, though she was not gagged.

Roy's right leg was tied to Mae's left with a wire coat hanger. A leather belt also bound their legs together. A small cord was tied around Roy's neck and came down around his arm, through his wristwatch, wound around his wife's arm, through her wristwatch, and up around her neck. An additional light cord was used to tie their arms together.

Rope and heavy packing twine added to the tangle of bonds that held the bodies together. Roy and Mae's hands and feet had been tied separately. The killer wrapped the two bodies together so closely that neither Hutson nor Ewell could see Mae's body in the early morning light when they entered the bedroom.

The rope, string, cord, and metal wire had cut into the victims' wrists, throats, and ankles. Under their chins were sheer undergarments and a man's handkerchief, untied. Another undergarment had been knotted about Mae's throat, and third one was used as a blindfold. An officer who lifted one of the silken undergarments lying on the victims' throats noticed a small damp spot and caught a whiff of what smelled like chloroform.

Later that morning, Hutson and other investigators spoke to Jo Ann, who in a shaky voice recounted the following...

Between the hours of 2:30 and 4:30 a.m., she was awakened by a noise and went into the kitchen to get a drink of water. In this first account, she went into her parents' bedroom, either after hearing her mother cry out or when she called to her mother and received no reply. She was started by what she described as "a big, bad man" standing in the shadows by the dresser.

She asked what he was doing. Instead of replying, he hit her on the head, grabbed her by the shoulders, pushed her down the hallway, and shoved her into the nursery closet. Before slamming the door, he threw what she felt was water on her, but it smelled funny.

She was overcome by drowsiness and stayed in the closet for the rest of the night. When she awoke, she crawled out of the closet, but it was still dark inside the house, and a cold wind was blowing through the open nursery window. Her baby sister, Jane, was standing in her baby bed and crying. Jo Ann silently crossed the room and lifted her out of the bed. The girls went into their parents' bedroom, but when

Jo Ann spoke to her mother, there was no answer. She reached out and touched her mother's cold feet.

Taking on her role as Jane's protector, Jo Ann said she unlatched the back-screen door and trudged down the street before finding Mayda Grissom at about 7:50 a.m. Jo Ann said to Mayda, "My mother and daddy are killed—bad man killed them." Jo Ann said the intruder was "a man with ugly round feet and hairy eyebrows" and that he "wore clothes on his head with holes for eyes and he wore gloves." Jo Ann repeatedly said the man did not say anything.

The sisters' nursery room had become part of the crime scene, with its scattered clothes, scuffed shoes, and a jumble of toys and picture books. Their lives had been irreversibly altered in the blink of an eye.

As reporters began gathering around the Hunts' home later that morning, Hutson told them that the couple had been tied, but by all indications, Mae had put up a significant struggle. He claimed:

> She had a bad head bruise from a blow which might have fractured her skull, but a more complete examination would have to be made before it could be determined how the couple died. This is awful and we haven't even gotten well started. It looks like both were beaten, as well as shot, but we can't tell much until technicians remove and examine the bodies.

Even those with hardened emotions and cast-iron stomachs were affected by the bloody bedroom scene. Upon entering the bedroom, police officers and crime scene technicians bent at the waists as if they were about to be sick.

Later that morning, Texas Ranger Benjamin Maney Gault arrived and took control of the investigation. Gault began his career as a Ranger in 1929, and although he resigned for a brief period in 1933 for undisclosed reasons, he was appointed in 1934 to the Texas Highway Patrolmen Commission, where he was part of the posse that tracked down and killed Bonnie Parker and Clyde Barrow in Louisiana.

Governor James Allred asked him to come back to the Texas Rangers to serve as a sergeant in 1935 in Travis County. By 1938, Gault took over as captain of the Texas Rangers' C Company in Lubbock, which covered ninety-four counties in West Texas. To friends and acquaintances, Gault was a twenty-three-karat fellow who was loyal and cool-headed.

Gault did not care for publicity. One reporter described him as a "cold-eyed, mysterious man who did not talk" and had "an occasional big smile, with blue eyes that could either twinkle or pierce." Gault always wore a plain, single-breasted suit and an iconic straw hat.

Throughout his law enforcement career, Gault helped close gambling establishments and worked on cases involving auto thefts, bootlegging rings, race riots, bank robberies, and cattle rustlings. The Hunt murder investigation was his first and only murder case.

People gathering on the street outside the Hunt residence spoke in subdued tones, whispering about the murderer possibly hiding around the house before the murders.

An eerie silence fell over Littlefield. Away from the flurry of law enforcement, reporters and medical personnel descending on the Hunt home, the town came to a standstill. Even the gins and cotton mill fell silent. The flag at the post office hung weakly from the pole. The story soon hit The Associated Press wire and stories about the murders appeared in the *Chicago Daily Tribune*, *Washington Post*, and *Kansas City Star*.

At the hospital, the door to Roy's darkened office remained closed. A small ray of light lit up a bronze plaque inscribed with the Hippocratic Oath "....and in proportion as I am faithful to my oath may happiness and good repute be ever mine...."

By the afternoon of October 26, Hutson and Gault realized that the murder case would be sensational because of the grisly crime scene and the small-town setting. Their investigation started with an obvious question: Was Roy's murder related to the attempt on his life the year before?

Hunt home in Littlefield, circa 1940.
Lubbock Avalanche-Journal Archives

Maney Gault.
Texas Ranger Museum

··· PART TWO ···

INVESTIGATION

8

EVIDENCE AND FUNERALS

Investigators processing the macabre crime scene gathered evidence inside and outside the home quickly, rather than following established procedures, which were more time-consuming, for recording and preserving evidence. Despite the horrific nature of the crime, most of the evidence was collected by that afternoon, and the bodies were removed four hours after they were discovered. Ed Watson, the Lubbock newspaper photographer, took fewer than a handful of photographs of the murder scene and the bodies.

Pre-investigation

By the time the murder investigation officially began and the house was secured, more than thirty people, from bystanders to police officers, had wandered through the house to glimpse the partially covered bodies.

With so many people traipsing through the crime scene, gossip about the murders spread like a prairie fire.

Investigators may have rushed through their evidence gathering because they had to steady themselves before confronting the horrific scene inside the Hunts' tiny bedroom. Most of them held handkerchiefs over their faces to quell the overpowering odor of blood and emptied bowels.

The Bodies

The officers investigating the murders had never encountered anything like what they now uncovered.

They started with the silk comforter, hastily thrown over the couple by Sheriff Hutson. A piece of white string about three to four feet in length was discovered on top of the comforter near the foot of the right side of the bed.

They drew back the comforter to reveal the blood-soaked bodies. Blood covered the mattress, headboard, and surrounding floor, and many other surfaces in the room.

Fred Janes and Ewell Hunt, who was also a doctor, examined his brother's body first, with Redwine, the Texas Ranger, looking on. The killer shot Roy in the head at nearly point-blank range. Redwine noted black smudges around the edge of the bullet wound, indicating the gun was so close to Roy's head that it caused a gunpowder burn. Even though it was standard procedure at the time, neither doctor noted whether the edges of the gunshot wound were blackened by dirt, grease, or partially burned powder grains expelled when the gun was fired. Nor did they note the shape of the entrance wound, which is often cross-shaped if a gun is fired at close range. They also did not mention the shape of the exit wound.

All that was concluded was that the gunshot wound was above the bridge of Roy's nose and a little left of center. Janes further noted that the bullet had entered Roy's head between his eyes, through the center of his forehead, and to the right of the bridge of his nose. He concluded that the bullet was from a small pistol. Ewell also noted Roy's jaw had been hit with enough force to dislocate it.

Mae's death was not instant. Investigators remarked that the only wound on her body descended from the right side of her head down through and past her right eye. The skull area around her right eye was visibly crushed, and her right eye area was swollen.

Ewell determined that Mae's death was not immediate because of the considerable swelling around her right eye, making her unrecognizable. Mae suffered contusions from multiple blows with a blunt object. The extensive swelling indicated she was still alive after she was beaten. Investigators speculated Mae was hit in the same place, probably by the butt of a pistol, and died from major brain trauma at about 7:00 a.m.

Texas Ranger Levi Duncan removed and untied all the cords and wires from the bodies. The insulation had been removed from the light cord that had been cut from a table lamp in the bedroom. Heavy cord ropes had been twisted and knotted around the Hunts' necks, arms, and legs. A single cotton cord of about three strands was tied tightly around Mae's neck.

Both Mae's and Roy's wrists, ankles, and throats had rope burns, indicating they had struggled against their bonds before dying. Roy had apparently been tied and bound first, and then his body tied to Mae after he was shot. They had both been gagged.

Redwine noted that Roy's arms were stiff and already showing signs of rigor mortis, while Mae's could still be bent. Based on this, Redwine established the times of death. Instantaneous rigor mortis occurs in cases of sudden or violent death. Normal rigor mortis begins about three hours after death, reaching maximum stiffness after twelve hours and dissipating after about twenty-four. Roy had died five to six hours before his wife, who had been dead about one hour before their bodies were found, Redwine determined.

The bodies were examined at the house on the small double bed. No other doctor, coroner, or investigator examined them later, and no autopsies were performed. The investigators, talking to reporters, dismissed any consideration that Mae had been raped.

Based on the account of the officer who lifted the undergarment from Mae's throat and detected chloroform or vinyl ether, investigators speculated that the Hunts and their oldest daughter had been chloroformed to silence them.

In the 1940s, chloroform was known as the "lullaby drug," and criminals used it to subdue their victims because it smelled pleasant and tasted slightly sweet, even though it irritated the lungs. This simple, colorless, almost deadly liquid posed the most significant risk to children. In those days, chemists were still not sure how chloroform worked chemically, except that it slowed the body functions and sedated the brain, sending a person into a stupor.

Chloroform was readily available in every drugstore and was often mixed into cough syrups or liniments, and was used as a sedative, sleep aid, and painkiller. It was also used to treat alcoholic delirium tremens (DTs), hiccupping, seasickness, colic, vomiting, and diarrhea.

About noon, the Littlefield undertaker arrived and took the bodies to the nearby funeral home. Pryor Hammons was the local mortician, and he wrote down his observations as he prepared the Hunts' bodies for burial later that day:

> Roy had a bullet hole in his head just between the eyes. Mae had a discoloration on the right side of her head and around her right eye. Her face was swollen and both eyes were bloodshot, particularly her right eye. She also had a scratch on her right arm between the wrist and elbow and there was blood in her right ear. There was a mark around the front of her neck as if some cord had been around her neck and not around the back part of her neck. Mae's body was still warm and not stiff like Roy's, whose body had turned cold indicating she died last.

As the funeral director, Hammons was responsible for filling out the death certificates. A physician would add the causes, times, date, and circumstances of their deaths.

Roy's primary cause of death was listed as a .38 caliber bullet to the brain with no duration, meaning death was instant. Mae's was listed as a brain concussion caused by a blow to the head, with a duration of immediate death. Mae's death certificate contradicted what Redwine, Ewell, Janes, and Hammons said about Mae dying hours later.

Any lingering evidence on the Hunts' bodies was destroyed by the embalming chemicals and the washing of their hair. Roy also was shaved. All traces of soot, powder, hair, blood, and any other trace evidence were washed down the drain.

Hammons cleaned their mouths, noses, and ears of blood. He plugged all their orifices and openings with cotton to prevent seepage, further removing any clues to their skull fractures. He closed their eyes with eye caps and wired their mouths shut. He filled Roy's gunshot wound with wax. The families requested open caskets, so Hammons gave special attention to the Hunts' hands, fingernails, and faces, removing the last traces of evidence such as blood, hair, and skin from underneath their nails.

Back at the house, investigators wrapped up their work in the couple's bedroom, the house, and the surrounding area before sundown. They collected no other evidence from the crime scene.

The most chilling evidence uncovered was inside and outside the children's nursery. The killer entered through the south nursery window, even though the front and back doors were unlocked. The murderer positioned a child-sized red metal lawn chair under the window, raised it, and used the chair to step up into the house. The killer then crept between the girls' beds. The dented chair bore a shoe heel print.

Investigators also found numerous footprints around the outside of the Hunt home, seemingly made by the same person wearing what investigators first identified as a pair of boots.

With his keen understanding of the importance of forensic science in solving crimes, Maney Gault was the first to notice the tracks outside the Hunt home. He ordered plaster casts made of the tracks outside the nursery window and in the alley. He gathered the Hunts' bedclothes to send to Austin for laboratory tests. Based on his observations, Gault determined with Sheriff Hutson that the killer may have been professionally hired to murder the Hunts. However, Gault never officially announced his assumptions.

Other clues indicated that the assailant had kicked down the southeast corner gate in the backyard, which was about thirty-five feet from the Hunts' back door, suggesting that the person fled the scene quickly after taking extensive time to bind the bodies so intricately.

Investigators collected pieces of the gate as evidence. They also found tire tracks in the alley behind the Hunt home and at a nearby laundry, but instead of plaster casts, they only made one drawing of the tracks.

Hutson and Gault parceled out clues to the media during the day's investigation. The most peculiar news came from Gault and other Texas Rangers, who had watched thousands of Texas calves tied for branding. Applying this knowledge of ranching, they speculated that a left-handed person had tied all the knots on the Hunts' bodies because the pull was tighter on a left-handed rope.

The Double Funeral

The couple was laid to rest on Thursday evening, October 28, less than forty-eight hours after they were murdered. Three services were held as final tributes to the couple. At the first service at 2:00 p.m., mourners began filing into the Littlefield First Methodist Church before noon, and the church filled quickly, with people spilling along the sides into the foyer and past the church doors, which were propped open. The crowd was the second largest in Littlefield's history, surpassed only by the 1,500 people who turned out for Sheriff Loyd's funeral six years earlier.

The couple had attended the First Methodist Church for seven years, and it now held their caskets in the front altar area surrounded by hundreds of floral memorials from all over the country.

Jo Ann and Jane did not attend their parents' funeral.

As the service began, delicate sunshine filtered through the stained-glass windows, like a heavenly veil covering the flower-banked altar and the solid walnut caskets.

Reverends C. Frank York, a Methodist pastor, and George Rogers, a Presbyterian minister, officiated. The men recited scriptures and prayers for the survivors, who occupied separate sets of pews. During the solemn service, the organ played "The Rosary," "Berceuse," "Prelude in C Minor," "Elegy" from Massene, "Ave Maria," and "The Prayer" from Finlandia, with the church choir singing "In the Garden."

As the service ended, everyone, both in attendance and those standing outside, lined up to walk past the caskets to pay their final respects.

Funeral attendants diligently stood guard by each open casket for an hour as people solemnly filed by. Newspaper reports stated a few wiped tears from their eyes. Other reports speculated that most came to gawk at the slain couple. According to many people who attended the funeral, Hammons did a remarkable job with their disfigured faces. However, it was still evident they did not die peacefully.

After the last mourner passed, the pallbearers gathered the linings, laid them over each body, and closed the caskets. They carried the caskets to the two waiting hearses parked in front of the church for a funeral procession to Lubbock.

Brief services were held at about 5:00 p.m. at Sanders Chapel in Lubbock, with Elder Liff Sanders of the Lubbock Church of Christ officiating. This pioneer preacher had moved from Lockney to Lubbock and was passionate in asking the Lord for blessings on the couple and on those bereaved by the tragedy.

It was atypical for preachers of that day to carry their passion into a sermon, but Liff declared from the pulpit that the physician and his beautiful wife had been sacrificed to the bloodlust of a fiend and reiterated that they were trussed with wire, cord, metal clothes hangers, and straps.

Family members and mourners traveled the last few miles to the City of Lubbock Cemetery, where hundreds of people gathered for the double graveside service. More tears flowed, and sobs filled the somber air of the cemetery. With the final amen, the caskets were lowered into the eternal twin graves, just as the sun was setting.

Visit Inside the Former Hunt House

During my research, I drove by the Hunt house more than a dozen times. It had been vacant often over the years, but its deterioration never seemed to erase the reminder of that awful event so many years ago. I have taken friends to look at the house, and one expressed surprise at how small it is.

When a fellow paranormal investigator said she would go with me to see if we could get inside the house, I jumped at the chance. Our mission was two-fold: I wanted a better understanding of the house in relation to this story, and yes, I wanted to see if any paranormal activity was tied to the house.

Lisa Alexander and I met at the Littlefield courthouse in June 2011 before heading over to the Hunt house a few blocks away. When we got out of our cars, she asked in disbelief, "Is this the Hunt house?" I nodded and replied, "Yes, it is." Lisa replied with a low whistle.

Walking up to the front door, Lisa knocked on a new white metal screen door. When no one answered; we walked around to the back.

The former Hunt house has deteriorated. The foundation has settled over time, making the structure uneven. Bricks are missing from the parts of the chimney and other sections. The back window where the killer entered the house was about three feet from the ground, with its bottom ledge at my waist level. With no one home, we left for lunch and returned about an hour later to a still-empty house.

We attached a brief note with contact information on the back door. I drove around downtown Littlefield before going by the house one more time. This time, a blue van was in the driveway, so I called Lisa and told her to meet me back at the house. Before we had a chance to knock, a robust, well-dressed man walked out the front door.

He introduced himself as Roy Smith. Speaking in broken Spanish, Lisa explained what we wanted. Smith said he did not want people coming into his house. A few minutes later, though, he said he would make an exception if we gave him $20 to help with gas to go to Lubbock. While Lisa and I debated, he raised his price to $40, and Lisa countered with $30.

Money in his hand, I went and gathered my camera. Another dream come true—to see inside the house.

Walking over the threshold of the former Hunt home was not as climactic as I imagined. My first impression was how tiny the house was.

Despite its size, the house had been grand in the 1930s and 1940s, with its art deco embellishments that were now in disrepair.

The front bedroom was to the left, just three small steps from the front door. When Smith opened the west bedroom door for us, I said, "Oh shit!" The room was tinier than I imagined from all the documents I'd seen, including the photographs. Lisa estimated the room was about ten feet square.

The bedroom had a double bed, a long dresser, a small end table, and a lamp. I was struck by how little maneuverability the Hunts' killer must have had in the room.

It was difficult to imagine how two people were murdered in such a cramped space, with a double bed, dressers, nightstand, and a chair leaving hardly any walking room. Even the closet was tiny. It could hold a few clothes at best. The room's only unique feature was that it had two entry doors facing south and west, and four glass-paned windows that allowed both northern and eastern sunlight into the room.

Other than the addition of a dropped popcorn ceiling, everything in the house was original, including hardware, cabinets, and doors. Many areas even had the original paint. A wood-framed, brick fireplace was on the north wall, with built-in shelving flanking one side. The original light fixtures, now broken, were still above the fireplace. The original wooden floors were covered in cheap 1970s carpet.

I went to the back of the house near the tiny kitchen that had a sink on the west wall under a window. An open bar area separated the kitchen from the dining and living area.

A small, narrow bathroom was to the left side of the kitchen. The original 1920s built-in wooden medicine cabinet was still in place, along with the original light fixture and two oblong cabinets above the tub.

Inside the front door, a white wall protrudes out into the living room. The area behind this wall, which connects the bedrooms and bathroom, was larger than I expected. The nursery and bedroom doors were eerily close together. Standing in the hallway, knowing that a murderer had climbed through the nursery window and walked only a few feet to commit the crime, felt surreal.

I immediately had more questions for my research. How did the person know which one was the Hunts' bedroom? How did the killer know which nursery window to climb through? If the murderer realized it was the front bedroom, why did he enter through the nursery window? Why not walk in either the unlocked front or back door?

We did not feel any paranormal activity in the house, but I did become nauseated when I walked into the bedroom where the Hunts were murdered, knowing what had happened there. Before we left, Roy told us he had seen a flaming red hand come out of the bedroom closet, and his wife claimed to have seen a dark solid figure wearing jeans and a white t-shirt.

As I drove away, my scientific mind started wandering. A luminal test would most likely reveal traces of the Hunts' blood deep in the grain of the wood floors and on the walls. No amount of bleach and paint removes all the traces of blood, no matter how much time has passed.

The nursery window of the Hunt home with the metal chair under the window.
Gene Preuss

The nursery closet in the Hunt home. Newspaper reports erroneously said the killer put Jo Ann in this closet. The closet in her parents' bedroom was about the same size.
Lubbock Avalanche-Journal Archives

Toy-filled closet in which Jo Ann was placed.

developed, the ex-convict was bas-   the places where the shoes and the
ing his hopes on the State's in-

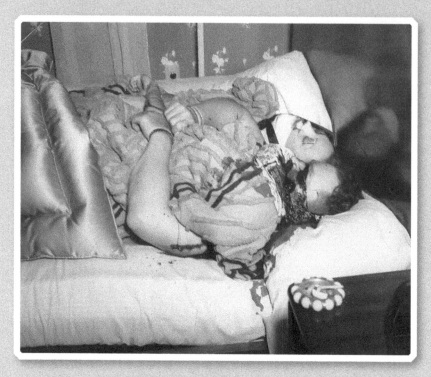

The south side view of the Hunt bodies.
A chenille bedspread covers the couple.
Gene Preus

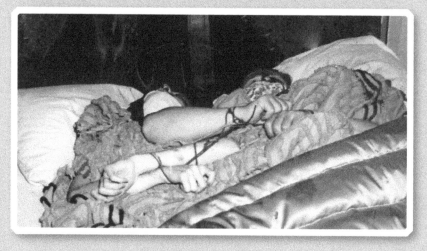

The bound arms of the Hunts.
Gene Preuss

A police officer making a cast of footprints outside the Hunt Home.

Lubbock Avalanche-Journal Archives

9

ALIBIS, LEADS, AND RUMORS

After the Hunts' murders, Littlefield became a community on edge. With or without foundation, many families were living in angst, terrified that potentially the same thing could happen again. In a neighborhood adjacent to the Hunts', some residents refused to stay in their homes at night. Others wanted to move. Residents locked their doors and viewed strangers passing through town with suspicion. The murders crept into almost every conversation. Families lived with the fear that the killer might return. Anxiety and uneasiness prevailed throughout town.

Newspapers declared the Hunt murders the most heinous in West Texas, reporting and sensationalizing every known detail of the crime. But two of the most important questions remained unanswered: who had killed the Hunts and why?

Speculation immediately turned toward the Newtons. After all, Billy Newton had been convicted months earlier of trying to murder

Roy Hunt, and Billy's wife, Ruth, was awaiting trial on similar charges. Oddly, neither Hutson nor the Texas Rangers initially investigated them.

A Fort Worth reporter asked Billy about the murders at his doctor's office in Cameron on the afternoon of October 26. Smiling, smoking a cigar, and sitting at an old-fashioned roll-top desk in his cluttered suite of offices over the First National Bank, Billy declared he had nothing against Roy and was at a loss about the killings.

"So far, none of the state authorities have questioned me regarding the murders," he responded. "I am terribly shocked. I am terribly sorry it happened."

Billy had a strong alibi this time. He was in Cameron, attending to patients. He later issued a statement about the murders:

> I never had anything against Dr. Hunt at any time and he testified he had nothing against me, so the whole thing is both terrible and incredible. I suppose it was the normal thing for the jury to do, to convict me, and yet I was not even in that section of Texas. My wife and I were visiting in the Sheriff's home at Caldwell the night of the Hunt shooting more than a year ago, and early next morning from Houston I phoned my office at Cameron. And everybody knows I was right here in Cameron when this last tragedy occurred. I think Dr. Hunt had real talent and was honest, but he certainly was mistaken in saying I shot him. I've been working here day and night. First, I knew of this thing was about an hour ago. One of my patients called me and said someone had told him Dr. and Mrs. Hunt had been killed. I exclaimed, "My God!"

He later added that, "My knowledge of Dr. Hunt and my testimony are all on the records of the trial. I have never had any ill feeling toward the man. I feel anything I might say now could possibly prejudice my case."

Talking to another reporter on October 30, Billy commented, "The killings were a mental ordeal for me. It is shocking. I have no idea what the motive was and then there are their two little children. I have three children of my own, two boys and a daughter." Billy strangely recapped his connection to Dr. Hunt to the reporter.

On October 31, Billy told reporters that he had sought a private conference with Roy after his first conviction in the roadside shooting.

"I wanted to find out why Roy testified I shot him, but counsel opposed the idea so I never talked with him, because Roy stipulated, I would have to admit I shot him and give a reason for doing so," Billy said.

Joe White, the editor of the *Cameron Herald,* noted that most people in Cameron thought well of the Newtons. "But because he was convicted," White said, "Their [sic] are some who think he may have had something to do with the recent deaths."

The first break in the case came almost twenty-four hours after the murders, when Sherriff Hutson and Ranger Gault issued an order for police to pick up a middle-aged convict in Galveston. When Hutson spoke to reporters, he said, "I'm going to meet state officers at Lubbock and bring the suspect to Littlefield to get him to talk."

Hutson revealed the suspect, Jim Thomas, would be questioned more for what he knows than for what he did.

"I have one million ideas on this case, but I can't talk about them until I'm on more solid ground," the sheriff said.

Initial Rumors

Rumors about the murders spread like wildfire. In Billy's earlier shooting of Roy Hunt, many in Littlefield speculated that narcotics were involved, but investigators could not prove the connection. Back in the 1940s, every American doctor operated under little-known federal law, the Harrison Act. Congress approved the law in December 1914 to regulate and tax the distribution, importation, and production of opiates and coca leaves.

Under the law, any doctor who prescribed narcotics had to register with the local Internal Revenue Service collector before they could prescribe or dispense remedies containing opium and coca. No prescription could contain more than two grains (grams) of opium, half a grain of morphine, one-eighth grain of heroin, or one grain of codeine.

A pharmacist dated every narcotic prescription, which also had to be signed with the doctor's federal registration number and include the patient's name and address.

With the Hunt murders, the local rumor mill kicked into high gear. Gossip swirled around bloody bed linens found wadded up in a trash can near the Hunt home—even though there was no report of any bedding missing. Other rumors involved the human hair clutched in Mae's hand, which was either a carefully guarded secret or never revealed by investigators.

Additional hearsay said that a strange woman had driven up to one of the Hunts' neighbors the day before the crime and asked which house belonged to the doctor and his wife before driving away. Chatter circulated that silverware and watches had been taken from the Hunt home and that the police had potentially found overshoes or boots worn by the murderer thrown through a window of a vacant laundry near the house. All these rumors became a long line of hearsay and gossip for the whole town trying to rationalize the murders.

Investigation

Less than a week after the murders, the State Department of Public Safety Lab in Austin issued preliminary results on several articles from the Hunt home that were supposedly released to Hutson but never disclosed to the public or reporters. For whatever the reason, Hutson leaked to reporters that the only fingerprints taken at the house were Roy's, not Mae's. This was odd because Mae lived in the house, and the couple had had frequent visitors.

Several days after the funeral, investigators began traveling all over Texas, following up on leads and credible clues. Hutson and Gault went to Amarillo, Waco, Temple, Houston, Galveston, Dallas, and Stephenville to investigate the leads they received in the first two weeks after the murders. Sometimes, Levelland Sheriff Ed Hofacket went with them to help pursue tips.

The piece of string found on top of the comforter was identified as evidence five days after the murders, but police never revealed how they connected that string to leads in Amarillo.

In Amarillo, officers searched what became known as the Veazey Garage and discovered a two-inch piece of string lying across one of the burners of a gas stove. The string was positioned in such a way that if the gas burner had been lit, the string would have burned. A few days later, they found a pair of tennis shoes in a closet of the garage's owner.

When Hutson returned to Littlefield after two weeks of his multi-city investigation, he was more reserved about any public reports regarding the murders, except to reveal that, "We are feeling all right over the investigation. We have a mass of facts and clues we were trying to bring together."

By the end of the second week of November, officers throughout the state had picked up several people of interest in connection with the case, but those leads became dead ends. The names of those detained were ever revealed.

By Thanksgiving, Colonel Homer Garrison Jr., director of the State Department of Public Safety, as well as chief of the Texas Rangers, said his officers were investigating two or three other men as possible suspects. He also said the DPS lab had completed processing many of the articles found in the Hunt home and in Amarillo. Garrison commented that most of the information, without doubt, pointed to a specific slayer, but he wanted to coordinate with local police officers to ensure all the information would stand up in court. Gault stoically commented later, "The case has to be worked up slowly."

Some people believed that the Hunts' killer was a fiend incapable of reasoning. Garrison, however, said he believed the killer was a professional. The murderer had worn gloves and a mask, carefully removed his overshoes before entering the house, and knew how to administer anesthetics.

Sheriff Hutson, absent from Lamb County after the first two weeks of investigative travels, made a statement in late November: "This investigation was being conducted all the way from Austin to the New Mexico state line, but it would appear we have little to go on—almost nothing tangible."

An unusual snowstorm hit the area on December 2, blanketing the flat region in a sea of white and creating drifts more than a foot deep. By this time, frustration was high in Littlefield and the surrounding region. People demanded more be done to find the cold-blooded criminal.

A lot of unsubstantial and frivolous evidence was gathered during this investigation, such as the weather report from the local COOP gin, showing October 25 was a sunny day, with sunrise at 8:02 a.m. and sunset at 7:01 p.m. The sun rose on October 26 at 8:03 a.m., with fog and clouds, and the sun set at 6:57 p.m.

In early December, Gault finally admitted, "This has been, and still is, one of the most difficult investigations we've ever faced in West Texas." By the second week of December, Governor Coke Stevenson called for police to search harder for the killer. He assigned Captain Hardy B. Purvis, one of the best and oldest Texas Ranger criminologists, and his son, L. Hardy Purvis, from their Houston office to work the Hunt case. The younger Purvis always wore a white cowboy hat and was always looking for bad guys. Gault, who had devoted what he said was countless hours and days to this murder investigation, expressed his pleasure at "getting well-qualified help."

By the end of 1943, no solid clues had emerged. Police had scant physical evidence, no weapon, no motive and no suspect.

The Reward

The Littlefield First National Bank established a reward fund to find the Hunts' killer. Funds accumulated gradually. By November 4, about $9,000 had been raised. One anonymous group gave $5,000. Lamb County Judge I.B. "Doc" Holt added $1,000 from the Commissioners' Court, while the City of Littlefield donated $500. Other notable contributions came from Dr. Alvin Borchardt with $500 (Jo Ann and Jane's uncle by marriage) and the Littlefield Hospital with $500. The Lubbock community added $5,000, bringing the total to almost $15,000 by the middle of November. It became one of the largest rewards ever offered in Texas to apprehend a murderer.

The *Lamb County Wide News* asked Governor Stevenson for a contribution from the state, but Stevenson urged state officers to solve the crime and pledged the cooperation of his office, saying:

> I do not feel the state should be asked to join in offering a reward. The atrocious recent murders of Dr. and Mrs. Roy Hunt, challenges the attention of peace officers everywhere. The solution of this crime calls for the utmost efforts on the part of state and local peace officers. The slayer or slayers should be located, arrested, and prosecuted to the fullest extent of the law. I have every confidence in the authorities who are directing this investigation. I commend those who are actively working on this case for the accomplishments thus far.... No clue or information of any character should be overlooked which would aid in bringing the guilty to justice.

Letters of Help

When the reward made the national news, Sheriff Hutson became inundated with what he said was about "Fifty to sixty letters a day from places all over the country," and indicated that he had not received "much of a lead from any of them yet." One, from an eighty-year-old soldier in South Dakota, offered an unusual form of assistance.

> I have read in the papers Dr. and Mrs. [sic] were murdered last week. If you will send me their birthdates, day and month, I can take my Bible and jasper stone and give you a complete detailed account of the murder, as if you had seen it with your own eyes. I have solved a large number of murders during the past fifty years for law enforcing bodies over the U.S. I am an old soldier. I'll do the best I can to help you solve the mystery and get the right party punished.

Sheriff Hutson boasted that he would answer the letter "just of curiosity to see how the Bible and jasper stone works in solving murder mysteries if the Hunt murder is ever solved." He never revealed if any leads came from all those letters.

Hutson also heard from mind readers, spiritualists, and amateur detectives, all offering help. "I think I'll have to hire a secretary to handle all the mail," he joked. "Practically all of the stuff isn't worth fooling with at all, but it has to be investigated like it is the same, in case there happens to be a tip in it."

Hunt Evidence

Despite all the miles they traveled searching for clues, investigators collected the evidence in the first fifteen days of the investigation. Ranger Redwine collected forty-six items from the murder scene and the outside of the house, including the items collected in Amarillo. They were sequentially marked from L-6782A to L-6782-TT.

All the evidence was turned over to Gault, who personally drove it to Austin and submitted it to the DPS's Bureau of Identification and Records Laboratory. Strangely, the only item not turned over to him was the bullet from Roy's skull, even though it was recorded first on the list.

Half of the evidence listed was not used in the subsequent court cases—not even the bullet. Where did the bullet go if it was taken from Roy's skull?

The items, cataloged by Redwine, were:

Number 1: One lead bullet removed from Roy's skull (caliber not noted).

Number 2: One ladies [sic] nightgown, one man's tie, and one pair of ladies [sic] panties—the latter removed from Roy's neck.

Number 3: One ladies [sic] nightgown and one man's handkerchief taken from the body of Mae—removed from her neck and mouth.

Number 4: Hair taken from Hunt bed.

Number 5: Electric wire piece from Mae's wrist.

Number 6: Wire from around Roy's wrist and looped around Mae's left arm.

Number 7: Man's tie taken from around Mae's neck.

Number 8: Fishing cord taken from around both necks of Hunts'.

Number 9: Billfold taken from dresser.

Number 10: Rope taken from around legs of Roy; it was cut.

Number 11: Cord taken from foot of bed.

Number 12: Articles taken from floor—covering from electric wire.

Number 13: Dirt picked up by a tree east of house.

Number 14: One bedspread.

Number 15: Fishing cord taken from Roy's neck.

Number 16: Size 12 child's pajamas.

Number 17: Man's leather belt taken from Mae's feet.

Number 18: Bent coat hanger wire from around feet of both victims.

Number 19: A piece of Kleenex.

Number 20: One pillow, two pillowcases, two-bed sheets all pink color.

Number 21: One piece of wire picked up from floor.

Items 1–21 were received from Ranger Redwine on October 29, 1943, four days after the murders.

Number 22: Man's tan colored sport shirt.

Number 23: Pair black tennis shoes.

Number 24: Three plaster of Paris casts.

Number 25: Hair removed from Jim Thomas hat, plus a piece of cord taken from stove drum at Sid Veazey's house.

Items 22–25 were received from Ranger Raymond Waters on November 1, 1943, six days after the murders.

Number 26: Hair removed from Jim Thomas head.

Number 27: Dirt taken from ground at scene of murder.

Items 26–27 were received by U.S. mail from Ranger Gault on November 3, 1943, eight days after the murders.

Number 28: Buffer wheel and samples of dust removed from buffer No. 1, buffer No. 2, grinder No. 1 and grinder No. 2 from Veazey's garage.

Item 28 was received from W.M. Adams by U.S. Mail on November 4, 1943, nine days after the murders.

Number 29: Sample of hair taken from Jo Ann Hunt.

Number 30: Dirt sample taken from a point behind the laundry in Littlefield.

Number 31: Metal child's chair black and red color.

Number 32: Six pairs of pliers taken from Veazey garage.

Number 33: One knife from Veazey garage.

Number 34: Wire samples found in vicinity of Veazey home at Amarillo.

Number 35: Two pieces of wood from the gate near the Hunt home.

Number 36: Pair of blue-green man's trousers left at Veazey home.

Number 37: Wire found at Hunt home.

Items 29–37 were received from Ranger Redwine on November 4, 1943, nine days after the murders.

Number 38: Substance found near a rock.

Number 39: Bottle containing a paint sample taken from right rear fender of 1941 Oldsmobile Sedan with Texas License Plate—F12-864.

Number 40: Portion of right rear fender of the above automobile.

Number 41: A brace from right rear fender from above automobile.

Number 42: Large rock taken from alley near laundry building.

Number 43: Two small pieces of rock found near large rock.

Number 44: Two pieces of binder twine found under Red Craig's car.

Number 45: One piece of binder twine taken from roll of twine found in Hunt home.

Items 38–45 were received from Ranger Redwine on November 8, 1943, twelve days after the murders.

Number 46: Blue colored man's shirt taken from Jim Thomas.

Item 46 was received from Bonnard Parker on November 11, 1943, fifteen days after the murders.

WILL JUSTICE

The Hunt Murders of Texas, A Mystery Within a Mystery

By PETER LEVINS

SUNDAY NEWS, SEPTEMBER 21, 1941

NEXT Monday, in Plainview, Tex., Dr. William R. Newton, 36, prominent Cameron, Tex., physician, is scheduled to go on trial for the second time in connection with the attempted murder, on May 21, 1942, of Dr. Roy Hunt, 37, owner of a Littlefield, Tex., hospital. In the previous trial, in August, 1942, Dr. Newton was convicted and got seven years, but the State Court of Criminal Appeals granted a reversal.

In the first trial, Dr. Hunt was the star witness for the prosecution. In the second trial, Dr. Hunt will not be on hand. He and his 26-year-old wife, Mae, were murdered in their beds on the night of Oct. 25-26, 1943.

Dr. Newton and Dr. Hunt had known each other for many years. They had been classmates at the University of Texas School of Medicine, and served their internships together at Houston. Both married girls who had been nurses in the Jefferson Davis Hospital at Houston.; Dr. Hunt had known Mrs. Newton before she was married.

Fotos above and below show the bound victims in their bed.

It has it say to the authorities, Dr. Hunt said that on the night of the attempted murder he drove out of town on what he believed to be an emergency case after receiving three telephone calls from a woman. At a lonely spot, he continued, he saw a large car in which sat a woman he identified as Mrs. Newton.

"You sure are a hard man to get," he quoted her as saying. Then she invited him into the back seat.

With that, he testified, a man appeared out of the darkness, an unidentified man, and, the doctor was dragged. "Don't you know that's a married woman? and immediately both barefoot and dressed in their night clothes.

"My mommy and daddy are killed," said Jo Ann. "A bad man killed them."

Sometime during the night, probably at about 2 A. M., Jo Ann had awakened and gone to the kitchen to get a drink of water. She called her mother, and received no answer. Then she went to her parents' bedroom.

She related that she saw a big man in the room. As soon as he entered, he grabbed her by the shoulders, pushed her into a nursery closet, "three waters on that smelled like gasoline," and slammed the shut on her. Soon she fell asleep, although she was lightly dressed and the night was cold.

Hunt Bedroom Was A Scene of Horror

Police officers, responding to Mrs. Grimson's call, found a scene of unbelievable horror in the Hunt bedroom.

Dr. Hunt and his wife lay on their bed in a welter of blood. He had been shot between the eyes; she had been bested over the forehead. The bodies had been tied grotesquely with straps, metal clothes hangers, tape, binding twine, lamp cords and shoe undergarments.

Investigators saw that the Hunts must have struggled fiercely, for their flesh was burned by the tight bindings. Apparently the intruder had tried to knock them out with an anaesthetic, and, this failing, had resorted to gun and bludgeon. The officers agreed that a strong aroma, noticeable in the room, was either used ether or tetryl chloride.

The fact that Jo Ann had mentioned "gasoline" strengthened the belief that some sort of anaesthetic was employed. The use of drugs, the officers said, indicated a person who had more than a passing knowledge of them, although their failure in this double slaughter hardly indicated an expert in such edge.

Needless to say, the people of the state were profoundly shocked. Within a day or so, rewards totaling $6,500 were offered.

Dr. Newton, who had been at his home in Cameron, hundreds of miles to the east, on the night of the crime, told reporters that he, too, was shocked. "I am terribly sorry it happened," he said. "I have just been reading about it in the newspaper."

He said he had been working in Cameron night and say, and that the first he knew about the tragedy was early that morning, when one of his patients called him and told him that Dr. and Mrs. Hunt had been slain.

"My knowledge of Dr. Hunt and my testimony are all in the records of the trial," he added. "I feel that anything I might say now might prejudice my case."

He refused to discuss the matter further.

The late Mrs. Mae Hunt

The late Dr. Roy Hunt

Who Can Figure It Out?

In May, 1942, somebody tried to kill Dr. Roy Hunt of Littlefield, Tex. A fellow physician, Dr. William R. Newton, was convicted in this case but won a new trial. Then, in October, 1943, Dr. Hunt and his wife were slaughtered in their bed. Dr. Newton goes on trial next Monday—but not for murder.

ing where he had been and what he had been doing for the past week or so, then laughingly had refused to sign it.

"He's a tough old convict," Hutson remarked, "and no hush when it comes to parrying questions."

Thomas' criminal record went back many years. In 1917, when just entering his teens, he served a t so for theft. During the prohibition era, he piled up a small fortune in the bootleg liquor market, and remained out of jail. In 1931, he got 25 years for a bank robbery in Nebraska, and served 10 years.

In 1941, while free on bond in connection with a robbery, he fought a gun duel with police officers near Lubbock, and was himself shot in the leg. Subsequently, on March 1, 1943, he was taken to prison to start a five-year sentence, but was paroled on May 13 in order that he might receive surgical treatment in Galveston. He underwent an operation to correct a blood system complication that had developed from his bullet wound.

He told reporters that he had lost 52 pounds in five days after the operation, and was "weak and nervous."

Incidentally, Thomas was able to discuss his operation in technical terms, for he had worked in the Nebraska prison hospital while serving his sentence for robbery. He had admitted to his children, he said, that he had been "a bad boy," but wanted to finish his five-year term and then enter business with a relative.

Sheriff Sam Hutson told the newspapermen that Thomas had willingly made a statement detail-

At the funeral services in Littlefield, more than 1,700 persons paid their respects to the couple. The bodies were then taken to Lubbock for burial, and there an even larger crowd turned out.

Meanwhile, the police had seized a suspect.

He was James C. Thomas, 49-year-old bank robber then on parole and living with his family in Galveston. Thomas, father of three daughters and two sons, arrived in Lubbock under guard at about the time the two victims were being interred.

Well-dressed and apparently completely at ease, he smiled when a reporter asked him why he had been brought to Lubbock. "They tell me that a terrible crime has been committed and they are investigating it," he said. "I don't know anything about the Hunt murders, and I'm quite sure I'll be able to prove it."

reported that they had enough evidence. Thomas was indicted, and was has just been tried in the court, the murder of Dr. Hunt.

DISTRICT Judge C. D. Russell presided; the prosecution was handled by District Attorney H. M. LaFont, assisted by two special prosecutors, George Dupree of Lubbock and E. A. Bills of Littlefield; the defense by Curtis Douglass of Amarillo, assisted by George McCarthy of Amarillo and Charles Clements of Plainview, former judge of the 64th District.

No Motive Established For the Hunt Murders

The defendant also had the advice of his brother, W. E. Thomas of Waco, a captain in Vaca Fire Department. Others on hand for the proceedings were A. G. Hunt of Lubbock, father of Dr. Hunt, and C. N. Franks of Houston, father of Mrs. Hunt.

At no time during the trial did the State attempt to establish the motive for the crime. There was no evidence that Thomas had ever known either of the victims. Even so, there was evidence, in the opinion of the state, that the right one was being tried.

Needless to say, the motive for a murder does not have to be established, although it usually helps immensely.

Thomas, large and rather dapper looking, still immaculately dressed and composed, sat at ease at the counsel table as District Attorney LaFont called his string of witnesses. As matters

Dr. William R. Newton

fired two shots. One bullet struck him in the shoulder, the other in the abdomen.

He said that he managed to escape in a field, where he lay low while his assailant, whom he identified as Dr. Newton, tried to locate him with the aid of an automobile spotlight. Finally he crawled back to his own car and, though bleeding profusely and close to unconsciousness, he drove to his sanitarium. There his brother, Dr. Exell Hunt of Lubbock, Tex., performed an operation which saved his life.

Following his conviction, Mrs. Newton had also been indicted but was delayed due to ill health; the defendant obtained a new trial on the ground of improper testimony. The higher court ruled that it had been wrong for friends of Dr. Hunt to testify that he had identified his telephone caller as Mrs. Newton.

Dr. and Mrs. Newton both had insisted, incidentally, that they were 700 miles from the scene of the shooting at the time of the shooting.

AT 7:30 A. M. Oct. 26, 1943, Mrs. J. C. Grimson, a neighbor of the Hunts, saw the two Hunt daughters, Jo Ann, 5, and Jane, 3, coming down the sidewalk to the Grimson home. They were

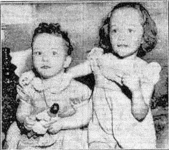

The murders made the front page of papers as far away as New York.

Newspaper Archives

Col. Homer Garrison.
Texas Ranger Museum

Gov. Coke R. Stevenson.
Texas State Archives

SENSATIONAL SPECTACLE

Time hit the brakes for the Hunt and Franks families following the murders. The days dragged into eternity. They still had no answers. No charges had been filed.

In November 1943, during the early days of the murder investigation, the second suspect in Roy's attempted murder a year earlier had her day in court. Despite Roy's murder, the case against Ruth Newton remained on the docket. The court still was required to prosecute her for the attempted murder of Roy's life in 1942. Even though Ruth's case was physically weakened by Roy's death, people expressed their collective doubts as to whether her case would go to trial, unless new evidence was uncovered.

After being postponed four times on defense motions of food poisoning, general sickness, witnesses in the service, and, in October 1943, because her husband's conviction left her emotionally distraught, Ruth's trial was finally set for mid-November.

The ever-prevalent winds ceased with fall's arrival, and the surrounding sandhills became still in November as the sensational spectacle began in the small Lamb County Courthouse.

Ruth's Lamb County Trial

On Sunday, November 14, 1943, Ruth arrived at the posh eight-story Plainview Hilton Hotel, of the Conrad Hilton fame, at about 7:30 p.m. She sat in the south lobby entrance, patiently waiting and looking off into space while her attorney registered them.

The following day, mayhem descended on Olton. People raced into town to get inside the courthouse and catch a glimpse of Ruth. Roy's murder had only intensified the public interest in Ruth's case. Rumors circulated that her first child was Roy's and that she was still madly in love with him. Spectators squeezed shoulder-to-shoulder into the gallery and lined the hallway outside the courtroom.

Instead of overbearing West Texas dry heat, it was a cool November day. Before the spectators could seat themselves in the second-floor courtroom, Texas Rangers frisked each one and asked if they were carrying concealed weapons. Luckily, none was discovered, and no threats were heard.

The Rangers never explained why they took such precautions at Ruth's trial and not her husband's. More than a dozen police and DPS troopers, along with Texas Rangers, were stationed in and around the courthouse, with the heaviest presence near the courtroom's entrances and exits.

Redwine and other Rangers attended the trial, as did at least three local sheriffs and other members of law enforcement. Noteworthy Texas Rangers present included Levi Duncan, Raymond Waters, Norvell Redwine, as well as Ed Sanders, a Sweetwater Ranger, and Dudley White, an Amarillo Ranger. Also present were Jerome Whitmire and T.C. Lewis, Department of Public Safety officers from Lubbock, and county sheriffs W.E. Renfroe of Bailey, Hugh White of Swisher, and Ed Hofacket of Hockley.

Throughout these abrupt court proceedings, the observers remained cordial all the while sitting shoulder to shoulder in the cramped courtroom. When the Newton entourage arrived from Plainview twenty-five miles away, Billy Newton wasn't with them. No Hunt family members attended the proceedings.

Ruth stepped into the courtroom more like a Hollywood movie star than a woman charged with a felony assault of attempted murder. She was accompanied by four lawyers and four undisclosed Cameron-area men, who would later pay her $15,000 bond.

Observers sat in stunned silence as they gazed upon the thirty-three-year-old woman. She wore a blue tailored suit, a jaunty blue beret with a white blouse clasped at the throat with a delicate butterfly brooch. As her staple accessories, she wore modest brown shoes, brown gloves, and carried a brown bag. Tiny, hammered silver pendant earrings adorned her ears.

As she walked toward the defense table, Ruth's eyes focused on the judge's bench. Composed and steady, she took her seat and looked straight ahead. Her beret tipped at an angle, covering the right side of her face and eyes. Ranger Gault sat down behind her on the other side of the railing that separated the gallery from the court participants. The only time Ruth appeared apprehensive was when a *Lubbock Avalanche-Journal* photographer walked past her with his camera poised to take her photo.

She turned away from the camera, lifting her chin slightly, leaving the photographer without an image. Ruth opened her bag but quickly closed it and resumed her straight-ahead stare. Three pictures were taken of her that day; only one turned up in the newspapers: a full headshot of her sitting at the defense table and looking down.

Occasionally during the proceedings, Ruth would frown slightly, furrowing her fine-lined eyebrows. A few times, her lips parted as though she was about to speak. Then she thought better of it and only nodded her head or gestured with her hands.

Of the thirty-six men summoned for her jury panel, four were excused for family sickness, farm chores, or being too opinionated. Ruth's attorneys came prepared to ask for a change of venue. As a safeguard, her thirty-five witnesses were at the hearing, ready to testify if the case went forward. The identities of those witnesses were never revealed.

District Attorney Harold LaFont immediately requested a continuance because military witnesses, Corporals Buster Weaver and Clint Fagan, who gave damaging testimony in Billy's August trial, were unavailable. Weaver was in an Army hospital in Massachusetts, and Fagan's whereabouts were listed as classified.

This became one of the shortest criminal court sessions in Lamb County history. Judge Clarence Russell granted with his own motion in instantaneous succession for a continuance and a change of venue to Hale County, saying that Ruth couldn't get a fair and impartial trial in Lamb County because of the publicity surrounding her case.

Murmurs swept through the gallery as Ruth and her parents were escorted to an anteroom off the court chamber. In an exceptional move for a Texas Ranger, Gault went with them. Finally, after waiting for two hours, Sheriff Hutson took Ruth into custody.

Spectators watched Hutson walk Ruth, unhandcuffed, to his car, placing her in the back seat. He drove her to Hale County and turned her over to the sheriff, where she posted the $15,000 bond with the help of her four companions. A few days later, Ruth's next trial was placed on the Plainview court docket for the January 1944 court term.

UBBOCK MORNING A

| Year, No. 11 | 12 Pages Today | Lubbock, Texas, Tuesday, November 16, 1943

Jap C. Bomb
Major Blow Is Dealt Balkans

Germans Threa Reprisals In Ra

By EDWARD KENNE
Associated Press Staff W

ALLIED HEADQUAI Algiers, Nov. 15—Tw
of American medium bom'
corted by fighters smash
way yards in the heart c
Bulgaria, yesterday in wha
ficial Allied announcement
the "successful opening of
kan offensive."

Official reports of the at
Sofia—first direct blow
garia since that country
war on the United States
1941—described the bom
"extremely accurate," w
Mitchells laying thous
pounds of explosives sqi
locomotive repair shops,
sembly shops, a main lir
and acres of trackage.

Nine Nazis Down
The Italy-based bomb
their Lightning escorts sh
dine of approximately
fighters that engaged th
fierce battle over the tar
raid on the Bulgarian cap
as the Germans were
using all available rail
rush men and supplies
the fighting in the De
islands.

"Through this immense
tant rail center, German
are transported to Gr
down into the islands
Aegean and also to the
Balkans," an Allied anno
said.

(The Germans broa
threat of dire reprisals r
ain for what they called
and undisguised terror
Sofia, in which many per
reported killed.)

Blockbuster Assa
The blow at Sofia, e
roundtrip of some 700 r
lowed by only a few
"blockbuster" assault
Wellington bombers fron
ater on a railway bridg
the resort towns of Ci
Monte Carlo on the F
viera, and a damagin
RAF Bostons on port it
and a chemical works c
vecchia, northwest of F
In all the Allied day
air operations only one
reported missing.

YANKS HURL BACK
SHARP GERMAN AT
ALLIED HEADQUAB
giers, Nov. 15 (AP)—
troops in the mountains
naap have hurled back t
counterattacks by refre

[Turn to Page 11, Colum

Allied Concentr
Hints New Land

[By The Associated
A large concentration
vessels in Naples hart
tive British minesweep
Allies are preparing t
amphibious landing
German lines on the
seacoast of Italy, Ca

rmy isolated
e Russia' yes-
striking dis-
erged on the
whose fall is

punched out
bend, in an
rap enormous
ld a German
but Moscow
fight entering

a Killed
flanking Gomel,
3,000 Germans
s, including the
mekhl, 34 miles
and only eight
titsa, said a mid-
roadcast bulletin
oviet monitor.

he Gomel-Kaln-
id highway, leav-
only one perilous
by railway, from
anning northwest
st line already is
y fire by Russian
north and south

killing 3,000 Ger-
teful blow north
shen, the Russians
s destroyed 40
aptured 27 more
ing order," and
reserves hurled
and captured 39
. ten ammunition
nd other booty.
'alish Border
northern Ukraine
ed a point 42 miles
Zhitomir to take
files from the old
d 150 miles from
sian border which
efore the Axis in-

oniy the Russians
on Korosten. They
15 miles southeast
il junction on the
sa line, and 25
theast, where they
orich-Khabnaya.
successes at wide-
ctors of the long
ered only by cen-
rman resistance at
southwest of Kiev,
he Rumanian bor-
way.

ured In
n Crash

s J. E. Boykin of
critically injured
moon at about 4
e car in which they
as in collision wh
uck on the highway

collision was caused
in truck attempted
er truck and met
r headon, according
Highway patrol
ly injured were Mr.

✱ ✱ ✱
Change Of Venue Granted Woman
Mrs. Newton's Case Goes To Plainview

By Staff Writer

OLTON, Nov. 15—Venue in the assault to murder action naming 33-year-old Ruth Newton, was shifted Monday to Plainview.

Judge C. D. Russell, presiding judge of the five-county 64th judicial district, which includes Hale county, changed venue on his own motion, after District Attorney Harold M. Latont and Special Prosecutor E. A. Bills had moved for and obtained continuance because of the absence of two vital witnesses.

New $15,000 Bond
Mrs. Newton, whose husband, a Cameron physician, was convicted here Oct. 25 and 'assessed a seven-year penitentiary term on a similar charge, entered with her sureties into a new $15,000 recognizance bond, which released her from custody and conditioned her appearance at Plainview Jan. 3, when the next Hale county term is convened.

There was no specific setting of the trial date, attorneys not having agreed on it late this afternoon.

The Newtons were indicted in connection with the May 21, 1942, shooting of Dr. Roy E. Hunt two miles east of Littlefield.

(Dr. and Mrs. Hunt were murdered early the morning of Oct. 26 in their Littlefield bedroom, approximately 18 months after the unsuccessful attempt to kill him, Dr. Hunt's death deprived the state of its principal witness against Mrs. Newton, and a procedural rule of evidence operated against admissibility in Mrs. Newton's trial of any testimony Dr. Hunt gave against Dr. Newton' if it tended toward incrimination of Mrs. Newton—since she was never accorded the opportunity of cross-examining Dr. Hunt.)

Main State's Witness
The district attorney informed the court that two witnesses he had relied on mainly in the case were in the Army, Sgt. Buster Weaver, ill in a Massachusetts Army hospital, and Pvt. Clint Fagau, whose location was described as a "military secret."

He said Cpl. Weaver—as he had

WHEN CASE WAS CALLED — Mrs. W. R. Newton, foreground, top, is shown in the district courtroom of the Lamb county courthouse at Olton, Monday, where she faced a charge of assault with intent to murder her onetime friend, the late Dr. Roy Hunt, of Littlefield, in the early morning hours of May 21, 1942. Immediately behind Mrs. Newton, and at her right, holding a hat, is Ranger Capt. Maney Gault, of Lubbock, who, with other officers, is investigating the later and yet unsolved murders of Dr. and Mrs. Hunt in their Littlefield home on October 26. Lower, Mrs. Newton, wife of a Cameron physician found guilty of a similar charge in his trial at Olton last August, is shown in a formal pose. Pictures are by Edwin Watson, of The Avalanche-Journal staff.

Spirit Of Alamo Sustains Texans Who Face Death At Bloody Salerno Beachhead

Ruth Newton on the front page of the Lubbock Avalanche-Journal.

Lubbock Avalanche-Journal Archives

ROLLING INTO 1944

As 1944 rolled in, police still had no arrests for the Hunt murders. Littlefield residents now routinely locked their doors and viewed out-of-town visitors with suspicion—or at least caution.

In January 1944, Texas Ranger Colonel Homer Garrison said that the Hunt investigation "is moving as steady today as it did the first few days and every Ranger captain in the state has the case on the top of his list. State and district officers have not relaxed for a single hour and the investigation will continue no matter how long a time is necessary until the case is broken."

Ranger Gault insisted they were making progress. "It is not possible for us to divulge many angles of the investigation at this time, but I can say we are not disappointed; we do feel the case will be solved," he said. "We expect to have a watertight case in every respect before formal charges are filed."

Life After the Murders and Case Developments

Officers insisted that the case was progressing and that they were examining every clue, but as the weeks dragged into months, it was evident that the murder case had stalled. A few people adamantly believed it would remain unsolved.

The only specific accomplishment in the case was the arrest of Jim Thomas, a resilient, left-handed, refined, middle-aged convict who cockily denied all knowledge of the murders. But he was arrested for a parole violation, not the murders. No evidence connected Thomas—or anyone else for that matter—to the murders.

Detectives, both professional and amateur, offered to travel to Littlefield to assist in the investigation. But in every instance, they asked for compensation or expense money, and Hutson never accepted their help or considered using the reward money to pay them. Many Littlefield residents wanted to employ a criminologist, but that didn't happen, either.

In reality, everything ceased with the case, except for the few words of encouragement to pacify reporters, who in turn occasionally presented updates on the investigation in newspaper reports. In their media statements, law officials said they believed more than one person—and perhaps as many as four people—were responsible for the Hunt murders.

Law officials indicated that their investigation covered a sizeable area of Texas, from the Gulf Coast to Amarillo, and while they said the leads they had followed all led in one direction, they never gave specifics.

By late February 1944, there had been no arrest and no charges had been filed. Jim Thomas remained in the Lubbock County jail after the governor revoked his parole. He had been turned over to the Texas Rangers, who could hold him indefinitely.

Apparently, many investigators suspected him from the beginning, and the Rangers were holding him until they could find solid evidence linking him to the murders.

In mid-March, the investigation took an expectant turn when the Rangers received a lead on the gun used in the murders from an unidentified Amarillo man.

The man said he had been given a pistol from an unnamed source. After having it in his possession for a while, he started getting anxious that it was stolen and perhaps had even been used in the Hunt murders. Because of his own criminal record, he feared getting caught with the gun, so he tossed it in the Canadian River north of Amarillo. The Rangers enlisted a county road crew with a crawler and grader to investigate the man's statement.

The crew used a heavy pump to divert water from the river to aid the search. An eight-foot-deep pool of the river's snow-fed water was drawn off, and the river's sandy bed was dredged for hours.

During the dredging, Potter County Commissioners and Ranger Gault were present. A Commissioner's hat was blown off by a gust of wind. Gault began chasing the hat and was losing the capture. "Shoot it," another yelled. Running at full speed, Gault drew his .45 gun and fired at the hat. The bullet hit about two inches ahead of the hat stopping it. "A great many things have been stopped that way," Gault bolstered as he handed the hat back to the Commissioner. No gun was ever found.

Despite the setback, Gault ended the search by telling reporters, "I'm convinced that we're going to get the murderers of the Hunts."

WHO'S JIM?

Jim Thomas became the only suspect officially identified in the Hunt murders. He'd been detained in connection with the parole violation charge in Galveston—more than 600 miles from the scene of the Hunt murders—in October 1943.

The Hunt Arrest

In my research, I found no reason why or how Gault and Hutson zeroed in on Thomas so quickly, other than he was a convenient suspect. Less than forty-eight hours after the Hunts' bodies were discovered, Thomas was transported to Lubbock for interrogation and arrested later, on October 30, 1943, for a parole violation for having left Galveston County.

After tracking Thomas to the Powell Hotel in Galveston, Texas Ranger Ed Sanders identified him by surgical scars on his right leg and drove him back to Lubbock. He was never officially arrested. As Thomas stepped out of the Ranger's car, he looked like a businessman wearing what appeared to be a new suit.

D. A. Harold LaFont and Hutson immediately questioned Thomas in a small windowless room at the Lubbock County jail, asking where he had been in the preceding weeks. Thomas repeatedly avoided or sidestepped parts of his story during his interrogation. After the first two hours of intense questioning, Thomas slapped the table with his left hand, "I have nothing to say at this time."

A reporter later asked Thomas if he knew why he was being held. Thomas shook his head and smiled. "They have just told me a serious crime has been committed, and they're investigating it," he said.

During a later two-hour questioning, Thomas, who had an eighth-grade education, dictated his recent activities, carefully establishing an alibi for the three days leading up to the Hunt murders. Hutson asked him to sign the finished statement, but Thomas chuckled and refused, nullifying the document's legal value. The statement's content was never disclosed, but parts were leaked to the public.

"This convict is a tough old criminal, and he isn't a boob when it comes to parrying questions," Hutson said. "So far, he hasn't satisfactorily explained his whereabouts during the days before, during, and after the murders."

Thomas had been questioned by police so many times over the years that he was a master at evasion and only said what he deemed necessary. He could be cool and emotionless, even under the extreme circumstances.

After these initial interrogations, Thomas was booked into the Lubbock County jail on a parole violation. The police report listed his property as $108.48, a wristwatch, a pencil set, photos of two good-looking young women, several snapshots of a uniformed sailor, and a dime-store greeting card signed by a young girl. Additionally, two one-hundred-dollar bills had been sewn into his underclothing. Reporters tried to capture a photo of the camera-shy suspect, but Thomas kept his face covered with a white handkerchief any time a photographer raised a camera.

Thomas was good-natured but was no stranger to tussling with the law. Considered handsome and with a soft-spoken Texas drawl, Thomas was described as a gentleman around women.

Seeing Thomas as a convicted criminal was challenging. He was known for wearing the finest suits, and his well-spoken demeanor and dapper appearance made him appear more like a businessman en route to a civic gathering or business meeting than a hardened criminal. But his brushes with the law included extortion, bank robbery, and attempted murder. The police and the Rangers saw him as a cold-blooded killer.

Born in 1895 in Waco, Texas, to William and Minnie Thomas, he married Cora Hancock, and they had two children, Adele and William. By 1930, Thomas was a merchant in Potter County and married to Addie Thomas, according to the U.S. Census. They had three daughters, Pauline, Mary Nell, and Jimmie Lee, and one son, Joe. Heartbreak soon followed when Pauline died in 1928 from pneumonia, and later, Jimmie Lee was murdered.

Tall, stout, and with gray eyes, Thomas served two years as a private in the Texas National Guard. Even though he had been a prisoner during World War I, he was required to fill out a draft card registration in 1917-1918, which listed his residence as a state prison farm in Weldon, Texas.

Jim's First Crimes

According to the FBI, Thomas used numerous aliases—J.C. Thomas, Jim C. Thomas, James C.Thomas, Jim Thomas, and James Clyde Thomas. He was investigated and deposed in numerous cases around the state. His criminal record began at twenty-two, when, in March 1917, he was convicted of property theft of more than fifty dollars in Nolan County. A month later, he was sentenced to two years in the Texas penitentiary after confessing to stealing over fifty dollars in three different cases in McLennan County and was granted a full pardon by Governor William Hobby in February 1918, after serving less than a year.

Thomas's McLennan County record reads like a gangster movie. While living in Waco, he was convicted at an early age of burglary and auto theft and served a three-year term in Huntsville. In May 1924, during Prohibition, a McLennan County grand jury found him guilty of possessing mash for manufacturing illegal alcohol and the unlawful possession of its sale. Five months later, he was arrested again for the same crime and for violating the Prohibition law.

In August 1926, a McLennan Country grand jury indicted Thomas for "white capping," a term for extortion and blackmail. He frightened three local businessmen—banker Chapin Seley, lumber baron William Cameron, and E.R. Bolton—with phone calls and anonymous notes threatening to dynamite their homes if they did not pay him five thousand dollars. A letter Thomas placed on the property of Chapin Seley demanded the money in fifty-, twenty-, and ten-dollar bills securely wrapped in brown paper. Thomas instructed Seley to keep the package at his home until told what to do next. In the note, Thomas thanked Seley, signing it "The Dragon." Police arrested Thomas later in Amarillo and found sticks of dynamite and fuse caps in his car. Thomas told the cops he intended to throw them under Seley's home if his demands were not met.

In September 1926, Thomas appeared in court to quash this latest indictment, which was based on the white capping allegations. He pleaded not guilty, and a jury acquitted him two months later after a witness provided an alibi.

Incapable of staying out of trouble for long, Thomas soon found himself under investigation for swindling in Amarillo in November 1929, and later faced a federal liquor charge in El Paso because he imported five thousand dollars' worth of liquor from Mexico.

Hastings Bank Robbery

By 1931, Thomas was in Hastings, Nebraska, and mastermining bank robberies. Before 6 a.m. on a cold early February morning, three well-dressed men entered the Hastings Bank by climbing through one of its windows. Their faces were covered, and they carried pistols. As bank employees arrived for work, the men grabbed them and took them to the vault. Then, they gagged and bound them at the ankles and wrists with wire and rope. The criminals stole $27,673 in currency, silver, and gold.

At the time, the Hastings bank robbery was the most impeccably executed heist in the history of the Midwest.

The robbers returned to their rented house a few blocks from the bank, where Thomas's pregnant wife and their twelve-month-old baby were waiting. Rather than leave town, Thomas, celebrating the haul, insisted on staying overnight to rob the other Hastings bank the next morning. His plan failed when the police tracked them to the house and surrounded it.

A shootout erupted, with the robbers and police exchanging fire as sub-machine guns sputtered, shotguns barked, and revolvers belched fire. Thomas was shot twice, but the robbers managed to capture seven of the lawmen, disarming them, and making them lie flat on the floor of the house.

Under the cover of darkness, Thomas fled with his wife and baby, using one of the officers as a hostage. They drove east of town with Thomas's wife behind the wheel, and she pulled over on a deserted stretch of road. Thomas stepped out of the car, and the hostage, Officer J.L. Ward Wood, asked if Thomas was going to shoot him. "I should, but guess I will not," Jim said, laughing.

Thomas wrangled Wood from the car, clipped barbed wire from a nearby fence, and used it to bind Wood to a telephone pole, leaving him unharmed. Thomas took the officer's .38 Colt six-shooter and tossed it into a nearby creek.

Jim, endowed with physical strength, was suffering from two bullet wounds in his abdomen. One had punctured his liver and lodged under the skin of his back. The second had entered three inches below his right breast. Police caught up with the couple a few hours later and captured them, transporting them back to Hastings.

"I hope I didn't hurt anybody in the shooting last night," Thomas remarked to a reporter riding with him. "If the officer the other fellows picked up don't get foolish, he will come out of it all right. We got a kick out of reading about the bank robbery in Wednesday afternoon's paper." When the reporter asked him how he was, Thomas quipped, "I haven't spit up any blood."

Police took him to the hospital for surgery, then moved him to the Adams County jail to recover. This took considerable effort because he had to be lifted up the stairs on a cot, then placed in the cell next to his wife.

All this time, Thomas called himself Robert Hendricks Investigators discovered the robbers' fingerprints around the bank window they had climbed through. Using fingerprint record comparisons and Bertillon records, they confirmed a positive match and determined that the man calling himself Robert Hendricks was indeed Jim Thomas.

Thomas refused to talk to Sheriff W.C. Condit, but when confronted with the fingerprints, he admitted he was not Robert Hendricks. Furthermore, officers soon discovered that the woman who had fled with him was not his wife, because he was married to Adele, who was still in Amarillo.

Thomas was moved to the Nebraska Prison Hospital and remained there for almost three months because of the damage to his liver. He was transferred back to the county jail in May.

Right before he was convicted and sentenced for armed robbery on May 9, 1931, he attempted to escape. He sawed three bars off his cell door using a hacksaw blade. The woman he claimed was his wife, who had been released by then, had smuggled the saw blade to him during a visit.

Jim broke into the courthouse treasurer's office and hid on a top shelf in a large pasteboard box used to ship auto license plates. Officers found him soon after, and he surrendered without a word or fight. He was sentenced to twenty-five years in the Nebraska State Prison.

Nicknamed the 'Tall Bandit,' Thomas arrived at the penitentiary in a three-piece suit, hat, and long coat. Heavily armed guards escorted him unhandcuffed. He may have done some hard, physical labor during his ten years at the prison, but he also worked in the prison hospital for several years as a trustee in the operating room, where anesthetics were used.

Investigators in the Hunt murders may have suspected Thomas because of his involvement in another bank robbery—this one in the Texas Panhandle town of Canyon a month before the Hastings heist. Thomas had a warrant for his arrest for this robbery.

This ingenious bank robbery began on January 10, 1931, when two masked men dressed in bulky coats broke into the home of Levi Cole, the assistant cashier for The First National Bank of Canyon. The men took Cole and his wife to the bank and ordered them to open it. As other bank employees arrived for work, including Randall County Sheriff John Fry, the robbers blindfolded, bound, and gagged them before taping them to chairs. The robbers walked away with almost $14,000 in gold, silver, and two thousand Indian head pennies.

Four months after the robbery, Ranger Gault was assigned to the case. He soon identified James Creighton as one of the bank robbers. Creighton confessed and said that Thomas had planned the job. Creighton had been convicted of murder in Missouri and was scheduled to be hanged, so he figured he had nothing to lose by confessing to the robbery. In August 1931, both men were indicted in Randall County. Creighton was not charged because Randall County officials could not obtain extradition papers for him.

Thomas was released from the Nebraska prison on December 13, 1940, on a commuted sentence after serving nine years and six months. Less than a month later, Gault arrested him for the Canyon bank robbery, though the case was dropped because witnesses could not identify him. Creighton's testimony was not considered reliable because he had attempted to gouge his eyes out after he was granted a second trial that sentenced him to life in prison. In January 1941, a judge granted Thomas's petition to dismiss the case because no other evidence connected him to the robbery.

Lubbock County Shoot Out

Thomas stayed out of trouble for almost two years, but in July 1942, he wound up in a pistol duel with a sixty-seven-year-old retired police officer, Baxter Honey. Just before midnight on July 25, Honey was working on a farm about a mile north of the South Plains Army Flying School in Lubbock County, where glider pilots were trained. Honey was at the farm to protect the Maitland Jones family after speculative, unconfirmed rumors that someone might kill Jones.

As he changed an irrigation line, Honey saw what he described as a heavy automobile stop on the Plainview-Lubbock highway, almost 200 yards from him, and heard a car door slam. Honey, who was still wearing his gun, recounted the events from his hospital bed, as a nurse fed him bites of his supper:

> I saw a man cutting across the grounds behind a shelter of thick growth. I moved across the open space of lawn to intercept him and find out what his business was. Just when I had reached a break in a row of young trees, a deep voice said, 'Stick 'em up.' Then the shooting began. I think the first bullet he fired was the one that hit me.
>
> I began shooting too. It was dark. The sky was cloudy and a mist was falling, but I could see the flashes of his gun, and I kept shooting at them. I emptied my gun and the man must have thought his was empty too. He charged out of the underbrush and we went together, swinging our pistols. I was conscious and having trouble seeing and, just before he came out at me, I could feel a sort of stinging in my leg.
>
> The fellow was strong and tough. He hit me a blow on the right side of my forehead that set me down on my hunkers. Then he walked off a few steps seeming like he must have figured he had another bullet in his gun, or maybe he found one in his pocket; he turned right around and came back to about eight feet of me and shot again.
>
> He must have seen the shot missed and I still was trying to reload my gun. He came in like a bull and we started swinging our pistols at each other again.
>
> ....I hit him on the head with my gun and down he went on his hunkers. He got up and I still hadn't been able to reload my gun. He walked off a few steps then whirled and came back again. We began swinging at each other with our guns. This time the fight just stopped, is about the only way I can describe it. The fellow just quit and went off. We had fought our way across the young growth and he disappeared in the darkness west of the lily pond and willow fringe and that was the last I saw of him.

Honey staggered back to the farmhouse, and Mrs. Jones called the police at about 12:45 a.m. Honey called the military police because he believed his assailant was a soldier. Searchers combed the grounds and didn't find the attacker; however, they did find blood on plants, a wire fence, and the Jones's private drive.

The next morning, investigators found blood in the field north of the driveway fence. They also found a hunter's corduroy cap and part of a woman's stocking with eye slits.

About 6:00 p.m. that Saturday evening, the Joneses called police saying they heard a man crying for help in the field. Officials came back and found Thomas in the driveway between the field and the scene of the gunfight. He told investigators that he was "Jim Thomas from Waco" and begged for water. He gave no account of the fighting. He had lain in the rain all night in the field, waiting for the driver of the car to return for him.

Thomas never gave a reason for going to the farm, and neither he nor Honey ever elaborated on the reason for their gun battle.

Surgeons marveled at Honey's ability to withstand the assault from the 220-pound Thomas. A bullet went through Honey's right thigh and out the back of his leg, and he had a cut on his head from a pistol butt. Thomas was hit harder, with one bullet striking him in the right thigh and exiting on the left side of the thigh at his buttocks.

In September 1942, Thomas was indicted for assaulting Honey with intent to murder, and a month later, a jury found him guilty and sentenced him to five years in the Texas State Penitentiary at Huntsville. The only evidence against him was clothing that put him at the scene. His motion for a new trial was overruled on October 7, 1942.

The walls of the Lubbock County jail became familiar to Thomas. He stayed there until early March 1943, when he was transferred to Huntsville. The long delay in transporting him to the Texas State Penitentiary was never explained. Two months after arriving in Huntsville, Thomas received a ninety-day reprieve because of his gunshot injury. He was admitted to the John Sealy Hospital in Galveston on May 14, 1943, and was operated on by Dr. Edgar Poth. Discharged on July 2, he received his last outpatient treatment on July 8.

Poth later confirmed during the Hunt murder investigation that he performed a routine operation on Thomas, who suffered from a peripheral aneurysm condition caused by the gunshot wound. "Had it not been corrected it would have meant Jim would have been invalid," Poth said. "The heart would've become enlarged as a result of being overworked in an effort to supply the normal amount of blood to the injured limb."

Thomas stayed in Galveston after his hospital release, reporting to Reverend Edmund Gibson, Chairman of the Galveston County Parole Board. On August 19, 1943, he received another six-month reprieve from prison. Gibson told Thomas he could not leave Galveston County under any circumstances without permission. Gibson later allowed Thomas to go to Waco for a few days, and he acknowledged to investigators that he knew Thomas had left the county two other times without permission, but he never revoked Thomas's parole.

Back in Lubbock, investigators grilled him for months about the Hunt murders. He often responded to investigators' questions with questions of his own. He refused to give any meaningful answers. If Thomas knew anything about the murders, he was not telling.

The house where the robbers were staying in Hastings, Nebraska.
Hastings Archive

Jim Thomas in Lubbock County Jail.
Lubbock Avalanche-Journal Archives

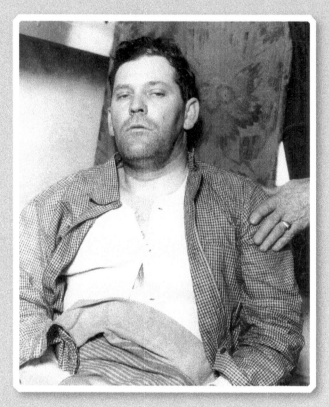

Thomas after being captured and before his surgery
to repair the bullet wounds in Hastings, Nebraska.

Hastings Archive

PART THREE

APPEALS AND TRIALS OF THE DOCTOR

IMPROPER EVIDENCE

The Hunts may have been dead, but the trials and troubles of Billy and Ruth Newton continued. For four months, Billy's lawyers primed his appeal of the August 1943 attempted murder conviction, for which he'd been sentenced to seven years in prison. Eleven Bills of Exceptions noting all the mistakes in the lower court case were filed with the Texas Appeals Court.

The initial appeal hearing was postponed in December 1943 because of the ongoing search for the Hunts' murderer. Right after 1944 rang in, Billy Newton's case came before the Court of Criminal Appeals at the Texas Capitol. His attorneys claimed that the Lamb County trial judge made critical errors, including failing to charge the jury, which is when the judge is supposed to explain the law that applies to the facts in a case.

On March 15, 1944, the appeals court reversed Billy's conviction. In their opinion, the two appellate judges, Tom Beauchamp and Frank Hawkins, focused on the telephone calls received at the Hunt home and concluded they had been improperly admitted during the trial.

Both judges pointed out that Roy and Billy were not friends, they had had no prior conflict, and there was no evidence that they had communicated with each other—directly or indirectly—after their school days. The court record stated that Roy and Ruth had not communicated, even though on May 19, 1942, Roy received three telephone calls from a lady giving her name as Ruth Newton.

The details of those phone conversations were not in the record, and the identity of the caller was established by Mae Hunt and the friends at the Hunts' house that night, who all said Roy told them who was calling.

The judges found credible Roy's testimony in which he stated he recognized Ruth as she sat in the car on the side of the highway and that he also recognized Billy. They also noted that other witnesses identified Ruth as the party who made a telephone call from the Littlefield Service Station.

But Billy had a compelling alibi. Witnesses from Cameron testified to his exceptional reputation and that they had seen him in town late in the afternoon on the day of the shooting, of May 20 in Cameron, making it impossible for him to reach Littlefield by midnight.

Testifying on his own behalf, Billy denied being in Littlefield on May 20, 1942, and denied shooting Roy, saying he had left Cameron between 5:30 p.m. and 6:00 p.m. for a Houston business trip.

The appellate judges indicated that if the state's evidence was reliable, and that Roy identified the Newtons, then the evidence of Billy's alibi did not hold up. On the other hand, if Billy was where his witnesses said he was, he could not have been in Littlefield at the time of the assault. The case ultimately hinged on Roy's certainty about Billy's identity, and Roy could no longer testify.

No one denied that a woman, representing herself as Ruth Newton, had called Roy, or that Roy went out to the scene of the assault. Therefore, the evidence given by Mae and the Hunts' guests about who had called Roy became important because that information corroborated Roy's testimony.

The question was whether that testimony was admissible and whether it was enough to identify Ruth as the caller. The appeals court found that the D.A. made no effort to support what amounted to hearsay as credible evidence.

Generally, hearsay is not admissible, but there's an exception if it can be proved that a statement was made naturally, spontaneously, and without deliberation during an event. These statements leave little room for misunderstanding or misinterpretation when heard by someone else. The state argued that "It was certainly permissible to prove by the State's witnesses, Ruth was in Littlefield the night of the shooting."

Mae had testified that when he hung up the phone, Roy told her who had called.

Nevertheless, Beauchamp and Hawkins ruled that the hearsay exception did not apply. The conversation between Roy and his guests in the absence of the appellate could ordinarily bear no relationship to the guilt or innocence of Billy. The judges scantily debated the question and further concluded that the doctrine of *res gestae*, meaning the events or circumstances at issue related to the hearsay evidence, was not applicable in this case.

Beauchamp and Hawkins were bound by the recitals of who, what, when, and why in the bills as to what had occurred. The judges' decision was devastating for the prosecution. Roy testified that he went to the place of the shooting in response to a telephone call from Ruth, but his testimony didn't show that he had explained this to his wife or his guests.

Because it deemed the hearsay evidence inadmissible, the appeals court reversed Billy's conviction.

Harold LaFont.

Christena Stephens

Judge Tom Beauchamp.

Tarleton Law Library, University of Texas at Austin

TRIALS AND SHENANIGANS

The state was pulverized by the appeals court's reversal of Billy's conviction. LaFont was undeterred. By March 1944, he was preparing to try Billy again on felony assault charges, although the process would take twenty-six months. Attorneys from both sides agreed to move the trial to Hale County, twenty-five miles east of Olton.

LaFont was also working on the Hunt murder case. Days before Billy's new trial, LaFont filed a subpoena *duces tecum* for all call records between Houston and Cameron on May 20 and 21, 1942 from Southwestern Bell Telephone Company.

Hale County Trial

In the final days of May 1946, Billy, Ruth, their lawyers and several witnesses arrived at the Plainview Hilton. This time, there were no reporters hounding them, no shouted questions, no bursts of flashbulbs from photographers' cameras. The night before Billy's new trial, the town was peaceful.

The next morning, people filled the Plainview's downtown square, mingling and talking about the case. Gossip was rampant. How would the Hunts' murders affect Billy's case? How could Billy get a fair trial in Hale County with all the publicity surrounding the murders?

By 1946, Billy's appearance had noticeably changed. His small stature had become stocky. Wearing a stylish gray plaid suit, he conferred only with his attorneys at various stages during this trial, speaking to no one else.

The courtroom on the second floor was packed wall-to-wall, with most people standing in the hallways or on the narrow staircase.

Jury selection dragged on for four days. Attorneys were exasperated when their aggressive questioning led to numerous dismissals. Two jury panels were summoned because most of the men in the jury pool had already formed their opinions on the case, along with a few jurors pleading for a release from jury duty. Out of the first panel of forty-four potential jurors, only thirteen qualified, and four out of thirty-four qualified from the second panel. Once the jury was seated, the trial began on June 1.

Billy's defense immediately argued for a change of venue, saying a fair trial was impossible given the publicity surrounding the case. Whispers ignited in the courtroom, with Judge Clarence Russell banging his gavel to restore order. He overruled the motion.

Little is known about this trial proceeding because the original court records in Hale County are missing. What is known is that Billy again offered his alibi as a defense.

Ruth was present at this trial, and she was listed as a defense witness. Also, in the courtroom were Billy's witnesses from Cameron and Temple, including his mother, Matilda. Roy's parents and brothers, Ewell and Homer; and his Uncle Alvin also attended.

The defense subpoenaed about eighty witnesses, calling twelve more than at his first trial. D.A. LaFont summoned the same twelve witnesses he had used the first time, except for Roy. Notable state witnesses included Ewell Hunt and Lamb County court reporter Dee Dodson, who read Roy's transcribed testimony. Only four defense witnesses were summoned, with Dr. Woodrow Avent testifying again for the defense that he had sought to consult with Billy about a patient, but Billy was not in Cameron.

After closing arguments, the case went to the jury on June 4. Jurors deliberated for more than thirty-six hours and were deadlocked at eleven to one, with one holding out against conviction. The solitary juror stuck to his vote, and Judge Russell dismissed the case without objection.

LaFont immediately sought to retry Billy in Hale County with another jury. Three months later, he appeared in court on September 21, 1946, requesting a change of venue because of the case's notoriety. Judge Russell granted the motion and moved the trial to Swisher County, almost twenty-seven miles north of Plainview. Ruth's case was changed to Swisher County as well. The Hale County sheriff took Billy into custody and transferred him to Swisher County, where he remained jailed until he entered a $15,000 recognizance bond.

Swisher County Trial

Nine days later, about a hundred days after the Hale County trial, and five years after the attempted murder of Roy Hunt, the state tried Billy for the third time.

This time, jury selection took two days and testimony began on October 2, 1946, in the Texas Panhandle town of Tulia. The courthouse was a three-story gothic revival structure with a clock tower at its highest point.

During this entire trial, Billy's mother, Matilda, sat beside her son at the counsel table. Her face remained unexpressive as the testimonies of both sides unfolded yet again. Defense lawyers continuously pointed out that no motive had been established for the shooting.

Ewell Hunt took the stand only to testify that his brother was dead. Court Reporter Dee Dodson again read Roy's transcribed testimony from August 1943, despite an objection from Billy's lawyers because no proper predicate was laid out for the introduction of a deceased witness's testimony. Judge Russell asked Dodson if the testimony was accurate. Dodson replied that he had correctly transcribed his notes at the 1943 trial. Judge Russell overruled the objection. Dodson continued reading Roy's testimony to the court as if he were Roy himself. Emory Camp read the Defense questions and D.A. LaFont read the State's questions.

Courtroom shenanigans ensued. Objecting to prosecutors' references to the phone calls, Billy's attorneys repeatedly climbed over the defense table.

Matilda Newton was called as a witness, but only to identify a single photo of Ruth offered as evidence, which the judge excluded after prosecutors objected.

LaFont asked Matilda where Ruth was on that day, and she responded, "I don't know whether I can tell you where; I don't know whether she is in Happy or Plainview or here." LaFont continued prodding her about Ruth when she replied, "I do not know if Ruth is physically able to be present in court or not, and I do not think Ruth is up walking around because it has been several days since I have seen her."

The other twelve defense witnesses mostly testified again that they had seen Billy in Cameron or Houston on the afternoon of the shooting or the morning after the shooting. This time, Billy did not testify in his own defense.

This trial had one momentous mistake that was only noticed after witnesses on both sides had given their testimonies. The indictment against Billy was not read nor presented to the jury at the beginning of the trial, nor had he entered his plea to the indictment charge.

After this mistake was brought to Judge Russell's attention, he meekly admitted, "We overlooked reading the indictment, gentlemen; it just escaped me the indictment hadn't been read." After dismissing the jury and then bringing them back in, the indictment was read, and Billy pleaded not guilty.

Judge Russell addressed the court, "The Defendant doesn't agree to anything being done and reserves our expectations we made this morning, but if it is the ruling of the court, the testimony can be reintroduced by putting the witnesses back on the stand, or we will agree the testimony may be considered by the jury as though it were reintroduced." Billy nodded his head. "I agree to that," he said. "Whatever my attorneys say I agree to."

Then, without explanation, LaFont introduced a 1933 University of Texas yearbook picture of Billy before the closing arguments, and defense attorneys entered another picture of him, claiming it was taken in 1933.

The afternoon of Friday, October 4, the trial's closing day, the courtroom was filled to near capacity. The crowd listened in intently as attorneys presented their closing arguments. LaFont and his assistant, Andy Bills, presented and summarized the State's case. E. T. Miller of Amarillo and Dennis Zimmerman of Tulia presented the Defense's closing arguments.

The defense requested jurors acquit Billy if, based on the evidence, they had any reasonable doubt he was in Littlefield on the night of the shooting.

The jury deliberated for two and a half hours before filing back into the courtroom at 8:45 p.m. A handful of people were at the courthouse when the jury returned. They found Billy guilty of assault with intent to murder. He faced as much as fifteen years in prison, but he immediately received the shortest possible sentence under the law—two years in the Texas State Penitentiary in Huntsville.

After the verdict was read, Billy's lips turned upward as he patted the backs of his attorneys and stroked his mustache, looking around the courtroom for the first time. In hushed voices, he conferred with his lawyers while spectators ambled out into the quiet darkness of Tulia's downtown square. Billy was taken into custody and placed in the county jail.

The next morning, his attorneys requested the court set aside the verdict and grant a new trial, but the judge overruled them. Billy's attorneys then apprised the court they would appeal. Judge Russell gave them ninety days to prepare the Bill of Exceptions and Statement of Facts. Billy was released on bond once again to await this appeal process.

Harold M. LaFont, left, and Sam Hutson discuss the
Hunt case at the Lamb County Courthouse.

Lubbock Avalance-Jounral Archives

W.R. "Billy" Newton.

Texas State Archives

Swisher County Courthouse.
Swisher County Museum, Tulia, Texas

15

AFFIRMATION

The Court of Criminal Appeals took eight months to rule on Billy's second appeal. While he waited, he touted his innocence to anyone who would listen.

The court delivered its decision around midnight on April 23, 1947. Billy's attorneys filed fourteen bills of exception, questioning everything from the impaneling of the jury and the reproduction of Roy's testimony to Matilda Newton's testimony. The judges were unmoved, upholding Billy's conviction. Judges Harry Graves and Frank Hawkins stated the following:

> W.R. [Newton} was convicted of assault with intent to murder Roy Hunt with the jury assessing him to a term of two years. The facts in this trial are the same as those set forth in the previous trial and appeal with some new facts and the admission of better facts, both relating to an alibi defense.
>
> The Judges concluded that the reproduction of Roy's testimony was admissible. Two of the bills dealt directly with other witness testimonies.

Bill Eight is of note was related to the ticket made at a Houston telephone office that offered to show a conversation W.R. had with an attorney in Cameron on the morning after Roy's shooting. Here the Appeal Court noted there was an annotation on this ticket at 8:48a.m. and on the back of the ticket were certain stamped places made with a machine called a calculograph that made marks indicating a conversation took place at 7:50a.m. This was shown without recorded objection. The witness was then asked by the appellant's attorney to explain how the operator could have made a mistake in recording this call at 8:48a.m. and the machine recorded the call at 7:50a.m. This witness was not allowed to explain under the objection that the ticket spoke for itself. The witness was asked, "Which is more accurate meaning the operator or the calculograph machine?" The witness was not allowed to answer that the machine was more accurate.

Bill Nine is exceptionally important because it complained of George Porcher's testimony. The judges carefully went over the statements of facts from beginning to end and found no testimony by Porcher.

This case based presented two horns of a dilemma. Roy placed the Newtons at the scene of the shooting, and witnesses placed Mrs. Newton in Littlefield just prior to that time, while an array of other witnesses placed W.R. at such time at a remote point rendering it improbable for him to have been present at Littlefield and committed this offense. This matter was presented to a jury and they have the responsibility of deciding from whom the true facts came, and under the law, we are bound thereby. We see no error, reflected in the record presented, in the judgment will therefore be affirmed.

Billy was dazed by the appeals court's decision. Yelling profanities at his lawyers, he raged at them that they reargue his case again to the appeals court.

On July 11, 1947, the court heard Billy's motion for a rehearing, with Dan Moody, a former Texas governor and Austin attorney, arguing some of the same points in the last appeal—questioning the court reporter's reading of Roy Hunt's testimony and arguing that the state did not prove Roy was under oath when he gave his original testimony or verify if the transcript was accurate.

The motion for the rehearing was overruled on July 28, 1947, with the court finding "no error in permitting the reproduction of Roy's testimony" and that "there was no error in the judgment." Not only did the court yet again uphold Billy's conviction, but it also ordered him to pay all the legal costs for the rehearing.

CIRCUMVENTING PRISON

Newton Board of Pardons and Paroles Hearing

With his conviction upheld, Billy did everything he could to impede it. He requested a thirty-day emergency reprieve because his patients' lives would be jeopardized if he went to prison, and he needed time to get his practice in order.

At a July 1, 1947, hearing, the state Board of Pardons and Paroles found that fifteen of Billy's patients were scheduled for major surgeries, and Governor Beauford Jester granted his emergency reprieve request.

In the meantime, the convicted thirty-seven-year-old doctor took one last shot and appealed to the board for a full pardon before he served any part of his sentence.

The board was created in 1893 as a two-member advisory, and the Texas Legislature expanded the panel to three members in 1929. The board considers applications for clemency on behalf of convicts whose sentences might need shortening. It cannot overrule the courts or set aside sentences before they are served.

Nevertheless, in Billy's case, the board on July 22, 1947, scheduled a hearing to consider his clemency application. The board gave no reason for its apparent overreach of its authority. Newspapers ran a story that Billy had been spending a lot of time around the Capitol in Austin—and not overseeing his patients during this emergency reprieve.

Alvin and Gussie Hunt, Roy's father and stepmother, his brother, Homer, Hunt, and D.A. Harold LaFont were all at the hearing to protest Billy's clemency. Ruth and Matilda Newton, as well as Billy's brother, Frank, were there to support Billy's appeal for clemency. In addition, state Representative Wayne Wagonseller of Fruitland accompanied Billy, who also brought *Cameron Daily Herald* editorials and news stories about the case to urge the Board to *right a wrong*. In all, about eighty people from Cameron came to Austin for the hearing.

Thousands of pages of petitions—containing between twenty thousand and forty thousand signatures, all supporting Billy—were hauled into the courtroom in cardboard boxes and presented to Board Chairman Abner Lewis. The board and Governor Jester's office also received almost two thousand telegrams and thousands of letters—more mail and telegrams to both than any other case in Texas history.

Jester's office responded with form letters to every telegram and letter. His staff even verified the names and addresses of each sender of all those letters and telegrams. Most notably, the staff hand wrote on many of them, "Not in directory" or "No One By that Name."

During the hearing, Roy's friends and relatives made emotional pleas that Billy's sentence be upheld. Roy's brother, Homer, submitted news stories and editorials from the *Lubbock Avalanche-Journal* opposing the clemency and vehemently declared that he had no doubt Billy was guilty.

> My brother, as he lay on what he knew might be his deathbed, told me and another brother, Ewell, that Dr. Newton shot him. He had no reason to name Dr. Newton's indispensability. When my brother

was shot down like a dog, his hospital was full of patients and they got along. At that time, neither Dr. Newton's mother nor the sheriff at Cameron could tell where Dr. Newton was. The mother told Sheriff Hutson her son and his wife were out of town for three days on business, but she did not know where to reach them.

Board member Richard Allen "Smoot" Schmid responded to Homer's testimony by saying that some of the clemency requests raised concerns that Billy could lose his physician's license if he went to prison. Schmid stated that it was "an unusual situation for your people [the Hunt family] to have to appear."

Meade Griffin, a Plainview attorney, who was there as a member of the public in support of Billy's conviction, conveyed to the Board that Billy had "nearly six years to get ready and he should serve his sentence. Otherwise, the people of Texas have a right to say the laws are not fairly and impartially administered." Then he added: "I personally knew Roy Hunt; I know he wouldn't lie."

LaFont recounted the trials, noting the Olton verdict was reversed because of the admission of hearsay evidence and the hung jury in Plainview. He described the results of the pretrial investigation, the questioning of witnesses, and that Billy had been found guilty by all but one of the thirty-six jurors who heard his three trials.

> "We have tried this fairly all the way through," he said. "It is a travesty of justice to even have to come down here and put this before you," LaFont adamantly stated.

After these impassioned testimonies, Billy stood to plead his case before the board, arguing his own appeal for almost two hours. In denying his involvement in the shooting, he expressed an unusual theory:

> "Roy first told [authorities] he didn't know who shot him. Then he told them he knew but wouldn't tell. Later he told them it was Billy Newton. It was an untruth, a figment of imagination due to shock and morphine which he admitted having given himself after the shooting."

Responding to a question from board member Strong, Billy replied that he "could not understand Roy's sticking to this story at the first trial eighteen months later. There's something in it I don't know. It didn't happen."

Billy called the pardons board as "the first unbiased jury I have had" and further implored them "not to send an innocent man to the penitentiary." He added that reputable witnesses proved his alibi for the night of the shooting, and eighty-eight percent of the adult population of Milam County and fifty percent of those in Burleson County had signed petitions.

Billy said that if he went to prison, his Cameron medical practice and training would be damaged and that he would be unable to care for his mother, wife, and three children. He further mentioned performing 6,600 consecutive operations without losing a patient and said he had given 330,000 medical treatments, more than half of which he did not charge for.

He even testified that Ruth's father had died of a heart attack on June 2, 1947, and her mother had already had a heart attack, implying that Ruth's father would not have died if Billy had cared for him, and adding that the "alleviation of apprehension is important in treating such cases."

During his plea, Billy said that Roy told a mutual friend, Ray Tallant of Dallas, that Roy would not press charges if Billy would make a statement about the case and "get him off a spot." In addition, Billy accused the Texas Rangers and other investigators of kidnapping one of his attorneys, Robert Lyles of Angleton, to obtain corroborating testimony supporting their case.

Billy concluded by telling the board he hoped to spare his wife and mother the embarrassment of publicly discussing the case. Something in Billy's demeanor changed as he uttered that last statement, prompting Schmid to rise suddenly from his chair and loudly declare, "I'm sorry if I caused anyone any embarrassment. I have just been sitting here and haven't asked a question." He walked out and did not return.

The board next heard from Ruth Newton, who appeared at Chairman Lewis' request, and she substantiated, for the first time, Billy's alibi that he was not in Littlefield at the time of the shooting.

When board members asked if she had called Roy on the night of the shooting, she answered, "Absolutely not." Her hands shook as she brushed away tears. Lewis told her not to get excited, to which Ruth responded, "Judge, this is pretty important to me. I can't help it."

Ruth acknowledged she had never been permitted to testify at her husband's trials on the grounds she was an alleged accomplice. She then stated the couple was together from 6:00 p.m. the night of the attack until 11:00 a.m. the next day. They left Cameron for Houston by way of Caldwell, where they visited friends until sunset and arrived in Houston at about 11:00 p.m. They spent the night in an apartment at the Sterling National Life Insurance Company Building.

Matilda Newton told the board her son was at home in Cameron an hour before sunset and could not have been in Littlefield, 450 miles away, by midnight. Reverend Frank Newton said his brother "means too much to his community to let a dead man's hand control the life of an innocent man."

Lewis, the board chairman, said the case was among the most difficult that had ever come before the board and that members needed time to consider the testimony and the protests of Roy's relatives.

Lewis later dissented and voted for clemency.

Schmid and Strong held with their majority opinion to block clemency and stated that the board "should not invade the province of the jury to determine guilt or innocence."

"The case had many unusual circumstances and if an error is committed, it is my judgment it should be committed on the side of mercy," he said. "Even if the doctor was guilty, which I seriously doubt, he is worth more to the people of Milam County, alleviating suffering and distress of her sick and in the field of surgery, than he would be incarcerated in the penitentiary."

Lewis said he could not believe all Billy's witnesses lied in their testimony to the different courts and juries.

"Some eighteen or twenty fine citizens of Milam and Harris Counties testified it would have been impossible, and he could not have been in or near Littlefield at the time of the shooting," the chairman said.

Lewis also noted the most damning argument: that investigators overlooked key physical evidence at the crime scene and investigation.

"With all the car tracks on the highway and shoe tracks in the borrow pit at the scene of the shooting, they could have checked, and investigators could have ascertained with a degree of certainty as to what kind of cars and tires were at the scene, and comparisons could have been made of human tracks," he said. "Any student of criminality would know the shooting was a hate affair, and yet both doctors agreed they had not seen each or communicated for nine and half years."

He also linked the shooting to the Hunt murders but argued that the community standings and family backgrounds of both doctors made Billy's involvement unlikely.

"Shooting to kill just don't happen in that kind of atmosphere," he commented. "It is my belief the person who shot Dr. Hunt on the highway did finally and with the same hate manifested it later by killing the Hunts."

To avoid jail, Billy needed the full board to recommend that the governor grant him clemency, and the other two members, Schmid and Strong, weren't swayed. They argued that the board "should not invade the province of the jury to determine guilt or innocence."

The board rejected Billy's plea for a pardon by a 2-to1 vote.

Eight days later, Billy wrote to the board in one final effort to get members to reconsider their decision:

> With hurt in my heart, but no hate, I will report to the pen with this valedictory statement. I will report to the pen Wednesday before my emergency reprieve is up to pay a debt I do not owe.
>
> I did not shoot Dr. Hunt. I have consistently felt I was a victim of mistaken identity. I have tried to keep my attorneys from saying anything that might hurt his character or reputation. He was a gentleman in every sense of the word as I knew him—may God rest his soul.

I am innocent and 81,000 good people of Texas have said so and 50 witnesses have sworn my innocent. [sic]

But the law has decreed otherwise and I shall abide by it.

Before I go, I want you to know I bear no malice toward Dr. Hunt's family. Feeling as they do, that I injured their son, I do not blame them if bitterness is in their hearts toward me.

The penitentiary holds no horrors for me. It cannot possibly equal the torture and torment of the past five years. There is hurt in my heart but no hate and no ill will toward any of the Hunt family. It is the prayer of an innocent man God bless the Hunts and you and guide you.

Billy wrote to the governor as well, declaring he was a victim of mistaken identity and recounting his plea of innocence. The night before he was to report to the penitentiary, Billy sent a personal telegram to Alvin and Gussie Hunt, Roy's parents. The contents were never revealed.

Smoot Schmid, a member of the Board of Pardons and Paroles.
Find a Grave

Texas Central State Prison Farm in Sugar Land.
Texas Department of Criminal Justice Archives

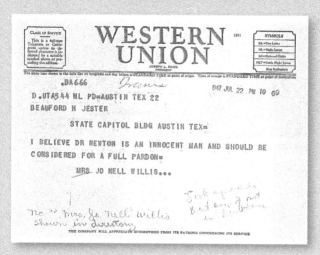

A Western Union Telegram in support of Billy Newton.
Texas State Archives

MODERN 58-ROOM HOSPITAL.....OPENED IN 1938

MEDICAL STAFF:
F. W. JANES, M. D.
J. R. COEN, M. D.
WM. N. ORR, D. D. S.

PRIVATE BRANCH
EXCHANGE
PHONE 301 AND 302

The Littlefield Hospital & Clinic

LITTLEFIELD, TEXAS

July 29th 1947

Govenor Beauford H Jester,
    Austin Texas.

Dear Govenor;
                I am inclosing an editorial in the Lubbock Avalanche
Journal of last Sunday which is self explanatory.We men of this
hospital were partners of Dr.R.E.Hunt and we have been fed up on
the inside workings of some men on the Pardon Board and some on
the Court of Criminal appeals.Justice has been aborted time after
time in the Hunt murder case and we are personally asking you to
request Mr Abner Lewis to resign.This man openly defended Dr Newton
before the pardon Board and it was evident from reading the papers
that he was a good defense attorney.We knew Dr Hunt and we know
he dident lie.He said Dr Newton waylaid and shot him on the night
in May 1942 and all but one juryman out of 36 men voted to convict
this man and the jury at Plainview in thier own minds knew this
twelvth man was fixed.It is a shame that this case has been dilly
dalled in our courts as it has.The people here have become tired
of the way it has been handled.I dont know what can be done but
we are determined that some move will and should be made to have
a more upright bunch of men in our higher places.We are makeing no
critisism of your 30 day reprieve but we want this man to serve
a term in the penitentiary and serve the full two years if that can
be possible.We hope this case can be presented to you in such a way
that you may render a fair decision.From talking to influential men
of the town it will be presented to you further. Please have an open
mind in the matter.

                    Yours Very Truly

                    Superintendent.

A letter from the staff of the Littlefield Hospital to the governor in
support of Roy Hunt and calling for Billy Newton to serve time.
Texas State Archives

PRISON WALLS

Billy Newton's Prison Time

On a humid, balmy July 30, 1947, night, Billy arrived at the Texas Central State Prison Farm in Sugar Land. Considering he was giving up his freedom, his demeanor was pleasant. Dressed in a blue suit, straw hat, and tan shoes upon his arrival, he soon was wearing white duck prison garb.

This prison farm, located on 325 acres, opened in April 1909, making it the state's second-oldest prison. It was immortalized in the 1920s folk song *Midnight Special Blues*. The song was originally sung by Crying Sam Collins with the chorus of the song, "Shine your ever-lovin' light on me"—a reference to the light of a train shining into a cell in the prison camp. The song has had various interpretations in the years since.

Billy was confined with ten other white trustees in this mainly black facility. He soon became a state-appointed trustee and worked as a bookkeeper, which gave him phone privileges.

Being behind the prison fence did not deter his efforts to reduce or avoid his prison sentence. Within days after arriving in Sugar Land,

Billy wrote to Governor Jester requesting a thirty-day emergency parole, which the governor denied.

In December 1947, Billy was transferred to the Texas State Penitentiary in Huntsville, also known as the Walls Unit. Straightaway, he learned he could reduce the length of his sentence by donating his blood. The standing rule in 1947 was to give convicts thirty days' credit for each blood donation and deduct that time from their sentences. However, each donation required approval by the pardons board and the governor. Governor Jester even researched the rules to personally understand the process for selecting blood donors in the Walls Unit because of Billy's frequent donations.

Out of the 5,700 prisoners within the system at that time, less than half were able to give transfusions, "and by the time all essential factors are checked in the lab, the number of qualified to give transfusions is even smaller," said Emmett Moore, warden of the Walls Unit.

To receive the thirty-day reduction for each donation, a prisoner had to maintain good conduct, which included being industrious and obedient. When blood was needed, the prison lab requested donors based on blood compatibility: "We try to give as many men as possible an opportunity to donate blood," Moore explained.

On January 16, 1948, Jester granted Billy a sixty-day commutation for blood transfusions Billy had given to other prisoners. Two months later, Billy earned good time credit of four months and four days. He once again became a prison bookkeeper, and reporters called frequently. In February 1948, he told one of them about his prison life: "I have been very busy. I have been going to bed around 2 a.m. and getting up at five. At the hospital, I help the doctors by doing electrocardiograph readings in heart cases and have been allowed to assist in some operations. The medical library has been open to me, and I have done a great deal of studying. All this has helped me keep my hand in."

A month later, Billy had earned good time credit of four months and four days. By this time, he was a bookkeeper at the prison. Reporters always called inquiring and checking on Billy often. Warden Moore said Billy had "a good record and was treated just like any other prisoner," and other prison officials described him as a model prisoner.

In March 1948, he again petitioned for a conditional pardon, but Governor Jester rejected the request for the second time in five months, saying, "There was objection by trial officers, and in line with the governor's policy, I'm denying clemency. I have sought the opinion of the original trial officers, including the judge and sheriff. I got no response from the latter two, and the Defense Attorney reported he could not recommend clemency. In view of the record in the case, and the lack of local support in the counties involved, I cannot concur in the recommendation."

Billy continued to use his status as a model prisoner and blood donor to reduce his sentence. He continued his letter-writing campaign, repeatedly asking D.A. LaFont to recommend that the governor grant clemency. In one April 5, 1948, letter, he wrote:

> I understand indirectly from Gov. Jester your refusal to recommend clemency in my case is the only reason he failed to grant this and he will grant it if you recommend clemency. He showed your letter to my brother which though it did not contain the word protest was construed as such by him.
>
> Frankly, I did not expect you to recommend clemency. Although, I was very impressed with your personality and ability by observing you at my trials I did not see how you could do this with the feeling as it was in at least one of your counties. I thought you might possibly be able to write a letter stating you would neither protest nor recommend clemency. Or perhaps you could fail to answer in case the Governor wrote you again.
>
> I do not know whether this is asking too much of you, but felt you would consider the fact I will have to take some postgraduate study before I can return to my work. This of course will keep me away from my business for additional time. You can readily understand the condition my businesses are in having been handicapped with this case for over six years now.
>
> Besides this I have a condition of health seriously needing attention. I have lost 45 pounds since coming here and have a great deal of trouble with my eye. I'm sure you noticed this during the trial.

I have five months left on my sentence. Would you if consulted again write to the Governor if you feel the decision on clemency is entirely his and you will neither protest nor recommend? I will thank you for an answer. If you can conscientiously do this I shall be eternally grateful.

In a subsequent letter to LaFont, dated May 6, 1948, Billy wrote:

I have letters from the Governor to my friends stating clemency was denied me because of your protest and you know the case and circumstances and have had an opportunity to determine whether the subject is worthy of the clemency recommended to the Governor.

Mr. LaFont, you prosecuted me efficiently and effectively. I do not believe you mean to persecute me. Would it be asking too much for you to write the Governor a letter stating you have no objections to clemency at this time?

The circumstances place my fate in your hands and make you personally responsible for my treatment at this time. I know the law did not anticipate this but the Governor's policy being what it is has this effect.

Had the Governor not taken his active stand against me, I would have been discharged by now on additional accumulated credits and would not have to ask for clemency. Therefore, I am not serving time over and above the court sentence which situation is attributed by the governor to protest from you.

I have never had any personal feeling toward you for prosecuting my case. I realized it was your duty. I do not know how you feel about it but I believe you fair enough to agree I should not be discriminated against.

Would it be asking too much for you to write the Governor you "have no objections" to clemency and you feel the decision should be his?

Billy said the governor cited LaFont's opposition to clemency as the reason he wouldn't grant it. His wife, Ruth, also joined in with an emotional appeal in a May 6, 1948, letter pleading for her husband's clemency:

Dear Sir—

It has been sometime since Rev. Frank Newton saw you regarding his brother Dr. Newton. He told me he felt from his conversation with you that you had no personal feelings against Dr. Newton and you did not object if Dr. Newton was granted clemency.

The governor tells me he is keeping Dr. Newton in prison solely on your letter you wrote him. I feel if this were modified the Governor would sign the recommendation. Would you please write him a letter now stating you need to recommend nor protest clemency in Dr. Newton's case at this time.

Mr. LaFont, I wish I could make you realize how desperately the children and I need Doctor at home. I have tried to keep our home going and the charity hospital open until he returns for he is the sole support of both. This community needs his services so badly. I wish you could see the tears shed by these old people waiting and praying for his return. I wish you could see the poor families he has treated for years without compensation who beg for him and need him. I wish you could hear my three small children begging me to do something to get their father home. Although you do not know these people or my children personally your heart may surely be moved with compassion for them and their needs.

The board of pardons will not consider sending the case over unless the Governor requests it and he will not do this unless you release him from the protests you sent to him. You see, Mr. LaFont, the welfare and happiness of so many hinge upon a short letter from you to the governor.

I appeal to you as a good Christian gentleman to help me and my children must urgently and humbly I beg you.

LaFont responded only to Jester and the pardons board, reaffirming his opposition to clemency.

In the end, Billy donated blood five times to prisoners or indigent patients at M.D. Anderson Hospital in Houston for cancer research. Prison records show each pint cumulatively knocked 150 days off his sentence. Including his reduction time of 232 days for good behavior. He only served 348 days—or less than half—of his two-year sentence.

The End for the Newtons

Striding into the warden's office before 7:00 a.m. on July 12, 1948, Billy greeted Ruth, who was waiting for him. They left a few minutes later after he changed into a light tan, baggy suit Ruth had brought him.

Eight minutes later, Billy walked out of prison a free man, having paid society "a debt that I never owed."

Before they drove off, he spoke with reporters:

> In view of the absolute innocence, this has been awfully hard to take, but I have taken it; asked no favors and have received none. I am going back now to my loyal friends at Cameron and resume my life where it left off when this nightmare began. Any man leaving prison feels a degree of humiliation; I know I can find my place again as a physician and surgeon. I have received hundreds of letters of encouragement; I will work to maintain the fifty-bed hospital I built and dedicated to the community before I was sent here. I have been fairly treated. The prison officials have been nice to me.

Billy also mentioned he had gone into debt because of his sentence, which cost him a 1,000-acre farm and five houses and lots. While reporters were still hammering him with questions, he grabbed Ruth's elbow, and turned them away, walking somberly to their car.

A few hours later, the couple arrived home to a heartwarming family reunion. His face was that of a jubilant man with his wife and children clustered around him. Yet he was nervous and weary. He was thirty-nine years old, and he had not seen his children since December 1947. After hugging each one of them, he happily listened to them trying to talk to him at once in their excitement. By nightfall, he opened the Christmas and Father's Day presents he had missed, which were stacked in the den of his eleven-room, half-century-old home. "This is all the big days of the year rolled into one for me," said the thirty-nine-year-old doctor.

His son, Turner, bought him a novel pipe, and another son, Billy, had made him a cigar box painted white with nickel-plated hinges. Billy's desk was piled high with telegrams from friends and colleagues.

Lighting a cigar, he inhaled in the woodiness flavor slowly before heading toward his massive gun rack that also held fishing rods. "Think I'll try out that lake of mine right now," he commented. "Not going to wait another minute."

Billy chose a fly rod and sauntered off in the dark at the back of the house to try his luck at his spring-fed pond stocked with game fish. He made about three-dozen casts, catching nothing. "I don't care if they don't bite. It's so wonderful just to be here," he boasted.

A twice-convicted man, he paid his debt to society, but one haunting question remains: Did Billy owe this debt?

Long after leaving prison, he continued to maintain his innocence, stating, "I had no reason for shooting [Roy Hunt]. He was a good man and a gentleman. I am going to devote my efforts towards clearing my name."

As for Ruth, LaFont reported that Roy's death precluded direct testimony in her case. "Court procedure will not permit testimony from a person who cannot be cross-examined," LaFont noted. "Roy's testimony against Billy could not be reproduced since the defense would have no right of cross-examination." Roy's statements as he stumbled into the Littlefield hospital after the shooting would have been the crux of the evidence in Ruth's trial.

The state never prosecuted her for her alleged role in the shooting, although her indictment in Swisher County was never dismissed. The only time she spoke publicly about the case was at the pardons board hearing, declaring "I never did call Roy."

··· **PART FOUR** ···

TRIALS AND APPEALS IN HUNT MURDERS

INNOCENT UNTIL PROVEN GUILTY

For seven enduring months, from October 1943 to April 1944, the Hunt and Franks families awaited any word on the murder case. While Billy's trial and imprisonment in the earlier shooting drew widespread attention, the investigation into who murdered the Hunts appeared to be at a standstill. Sheriff Hutson and Ranger Gault offered little hope that the killer would be caught.

Meanwhile, time passed slowly for Jim Thomas, who remained in the Lubbock County Jail under a parole violation for leaving Galveston County. His solitude was interrupted only when Hutson and the Rangers took him into an interrogation room and questioned him dozens of times regarding the Hunt murders. With every interrogation, except for Thomas's laughter, investigators left with nothing.

Thomas's reputation as a dangerous gunman seemed worse than his actual demeanor among officers. With a businessman's appearance, he knew how to confound officers by detailing certain aspects regarding his activities.

In a nutshell, investigators' frustrations came to the logical fact that in all criminal cases, the accused is presumed innocent until their guilt is established by a jury through legal, competent evidence.

Anyone can be tried for a crime, even if no motive is proven. The law does not require proof of motive to charge someone. An indictment is not an affirmation of their guilt. It is only a written accusation made by a district attorney who submits it to a grand jury, which then ascertains if sufficient grounds exist to justify a jury trial against the accused.

Grand Jury Process

A grand jury, behind closed doors to the public, calls witnesses, listens to their testimonies, and then decides if the case should stand trial. This panel returns what is called either a true or not a true bill. A true bill certifies probable cause, justifying a jury trial.

During grand jury deliberations, district attorneys may examine witnesses, but they cannot influence any deliberations, although sometimes their attitude can sway jurors. In the end, jurors must form their own opinions based on the evidence presented.

Lamb County Grand Jury

In a secret move, a Lamb County grand jury was finally impaneled in February 1944 to investigate the Hunt murders. Given all the alleged evidence gathered in the case, it was ambiguous why it took five months to convene one. Hutson and Gault hoped the jury would find the evidence compelling enough to indict Thomas.

When Thomas heard about this development, he emphatically requested permission to testify. The following is the statement of the only time Thomas spoke about the Hunt murders:

> I, Jim Thomas make this voluntary statement to the grand jury of Lamb County, Texas and to Harold LaFont, District Attorney. I have been living in a Galveston. I will be 49 years old in March. I am not married at this time. I've been married twice and have four children my youngest child lives in Waco with my sister. I have been to the pen

and the last time was sent from Lubbock County and got five years in the pen. I feel like I was not guilty of that offense.

I had been in the pen in Nebraska prior for bank robbery. I served 10 years on a 25 years term. I was in the pen in Texas in 1916 for auto theft. I do not know Dr. Hunt or Dr. Newton.

On Thursday, October 21 I believe it was I left Galveston and got into Waco that night and spent the night there. I called Marie Hall before I left Galveston and told her I was going fishing. I then caught a train and went to Amarillo. I got into Amarillo about 10:30 in the evening and went to Sid Veazey's. I stayed Saturday night at Veazey's and then the next night.

I used the Veazey car on Sunday afternoon and got back there around 11 o'clock that night. On the next day I used Craig's car and got the car between 6:00 and 7:00p.m. I went to the home of the married woman that night and stayed there until about 1:30 and then left and went out to Veazey's house and found both doors locked. I went back to the Angelus Hotel and tried to get a room. I could not get a room and I parked the car in front of the hotel. I went in the coffee shop and got some coffee and went back to the car and slept in the car until about 6a.m. I then went back to the coffee shop and got some coffee and perhaps doughnuts. I stayed around there for a while reading the papers and then I went out to Mrs. Veazey's house and when I got there they were eating breakfast. Mrs. Veazey had made comments about where I had stayed and I said you had locked me out last night.

She said she did hear someone at the door and I think she said she went to the door and when she got there no one was there. I stayed around Veazey's home that day into the afternoon.

I do not recall having any conversation with Red Craig about the killing of Dr. Hunt. Red did take me from Veazey's home on Tuesday night October 26, 1943 to Childress and nothing was said about my getting him into trouble about using his car. I wanted to go by Childress to see a gambler by the name of Goble Williams who owes me some money, but when I got there the bus was ready to leave out and I got on it and rode to Dallas by bus. I did call Marie Hall at Vernon I think it was.

Before I left Veazey's house on the afternoon of October 26, 1943, I got a call from a friend whose name I refuse to reveal who told me they were looking for me in connection with the murder in Littlefield. When I called Marie Hall after getting to Vernon I asked her if anyone wanted me and she said yes, the sheriff wants to see you. I told her I would be there the next morning.

I did not leave Amarillo on Sunday night or Monday night and I was not in Littlefield on either night. It has been about 13 years since I was in Littlefield.

I have known this woman in Amarillo sometime. I cannot tell her name as it would ruin her and her children if it were known she was associated with me. I have my record and it would ruin her.

The day before I left Galveston on my last trip to Amarillo I was robbed of about $460. Someone took it out of my pants pockets. They did not get the check for $165 I had of Red's. He had paid me for work I had done on his apartment in Amarillo.

I made this last trip to see this woman in Amarillo and to get the money on this check. I did not expect to be back up there for a long time as I had told my parole officer. I would do what he had suggested and stay in Galveston and take a job there than go to Amarillo and work at Pantex. I had talked to him about going up there and asked him if he would transfer me to Amarillo.

The grand jurors also heard from various investigators and eleven witnesses, including six who placed Thomas in Amarillo before and after the murders.

These grand jury testimonies revealed that Thomas was liked and trusted enough by the friends he stayed with because they loaned him their cars without hesitation. However, no friend could testify whether Thomas was right- or left-handed.

Sid Veazey testified that Thomas stayed with him during September and the days before the murders and noted that he was not as talkative after he returned on October 23.

Eva Veazey verified Thomas was in Amarillo before and after the murders and answered questions about the clothes found at her home.

She said Thomas had not stayed on the night of October 25, but she did see him the next morning when he asked for a cup of coffee and told her she had locked him out the previous night. He mentioned to her that he had a train ticket and said he was going home and was not supposed to be out of the county. She asked him why he was there. He walked away, not answering.

As to the clothes, Mrs. Veazey said Thomas washed a shirt at her house on Tuesday and hung it on the line. She found a pair of worn trousers and a shirt folded up in a closet and sent the trousers out for laundry. She also noted that officers found her son's basketball shoes in his closet and still had them in their possession.

G. A. "Red" Craig testified that Jim dropped by his house on October 24 and asked to borrow his car. Jim picked up the car at about 6:00 p.m. and returned it the next morning at about 10:00 a.m. He wanted to ride to Childress with Red. During the trip, Craig asked him whether he had done anything to get him or his wife in trouble. Craig admitted that he threw his own personal gun in the Canadian River two weeks after he was first questioned in 1943. The river was about sixteen miles north of Amarillo. Craig apparently kept the gun in his apartment, where Thomas had access to it and could have retrieved the weapon, but he never declared the gun's caliber.

Craig's wife, Irene, testified that she saw Thomas at their apartment before and after the murders. Thomas borrowed her car between 6:00 p.m. and 7:00 p.m. on Monday, and she saw him again the next morning.

Irene stated Thomas came back to the apartment during the night, but no light was on, so he went to Mrs. Veazey's and found her doors locked. He called Mrs. Veazey, and she said she would get up and let him in. Thomas said he slept there the rest of the night. At about 12:30 a.m., Louise Cantrell called the Craigs' and said she wanted to come to their apartment. The Craigs sat up with her until about 4:00 a.m.

During her testimony, Irene said the silver trimming along the right rear running board of her car had been torn loose, and the board had pulled away from the car. She admitted not noticing until officers asked her what had caused the damage.

Cantrell, who was at the Craigs' apartment on October 25 after a fight with her husband, testified that she saw Thomas on October 26 because he remarked to her that "it looks like someone has been treating you a little rough." She responded, "That is right."

Margaret Gaither was working at the Angelus Hotel coffee shop on the morning of October 26, and she testified that Thomas came into the shop at about 5:30 a.m., ate some doughnuts, and drank either coffee or milk. She noticed he looked worn and exhausted. When she asked about his appearance, he told her he had been operated on for a leg injury.

Marie Hall, a Galveston resident who had known Thomas since she was eleven, testified to the phone call she received from him on October 26.

Oddly, Robert Lyles, an Angleton, Texas lawyer, testified that he represented Billy Newton in August and investigated the first shooting of Roy Hunt. He stated that Roy had no enemies and was spotless as a hound's tooth. He determined no reason for Hunt's shooting or murder "because the way the crime was committed out here.... and the ways the bodies were tied, I have concluded it was the act of some maniac."

Eddie Glass, the owner of a downtown Littlefield café, testified he saw Thomas in his café on both nights of October 24 and 25. Thomas had come in, washed his hands, ordered coffee, and ate nothing. Glass said Thomas was dressed in coveralls or work clothes. He noticed his eyes had a malicious look, and he favored his right side when he walked. He stated he later saw Thomas at the Lubbock jail and that Thomas was the man in his café, to the best of his recognition.

Based on these testimonies and without any other physical evidence presented, the grand jury on April 10, 1944, indicted Thomas for Roy's murder. Nothing referenced an indictment for Mae's murder.

A warrant was issued on April 12, and Thomas was formally arrested at the Lubbock County jail for the murder of Roy Hunt. His reaction was "just what you would have expected," said a jail official.

"When he was handed his morning paper, he sorta grinned and pointed to his picture, holding up the paper so the other fellows in his cell could see what he was reading."

Another five months passed by before Thomas was brought to the Lamb County Courthouse in Olton, where he entered his not guilty plea. His attorneys requested a change of venue, which was granted because of the case's notoriety and the difficulty of sitting a jury. The case was moved to Hale County, and Jim was transferred that same day to Plainview.

By this time, LaFont and the Texas Rangers believed the evidence obtained thus far was only circumstantial, not conclusive. Rumors circulated that the strongest piece of irrefutable evidence was the footprint cast from outside the Hunts' home.

Sid and Eva Veazey.
Find a Grave

MISCONDUCT AND RETRYING

Thomas's First Trial in Hale County

As the seasons come and went over the course of nearly a year since the Hunt murders, Thomas's trial began on August 28, 1944, in the Panhandle town of Plainview. The proceedings garnered more attention than any trial ever held in the region. Vehicles crammed the normally quiet streets and people swarmed inside and outside the Hale County Courthouse.

The Hunt and Franks families wanted to hear first-hand the evidence investigators had compiled in the murders of Roy and Mae. A special venire of 136 men was called to the three-story courthouse for jury duty in Judge Russell's court. Twenty-four were excused for various reasons. Sitting this jury became an all-day and night process, with the last juror selected right before midnight.

During the jury selection, people were packed wall-to-wall in the courtroom, and they spilled over into the courthouse halls and staircase. Right before the trial began, Sheriff Hutson spouted to a group of reporters on the courthouse lawn, "The State has a much better prepared case than he expected."

This trial lasted only three days.

Thomas appeared in court clean-shaven, dapper, and well-groomed. Dressed in a blue pinstriped business suit, with a white shirt and a blue floral tie, it was hard to differentiate him from his defense attorneys. During the trial's opening proceedings, Thomas frequently flashed his dashing smile.

Thomas's brother, Wilburn, a fire department captain at Waco, and his brother-in-law, Sam Armstrong, a dry goods broker in Waco, were both in the galley.

Thomas's defense summoned only five witnesses; prosecutors called thirty, including twenty-one that testified about the forensics. Testimony was given on the pieces of string, a Lee tire, a plaster cast of a shoe track, and coat hangers. A shirt, trousers, and a pair of tennis shoes were introduced into evidence.

Putting everything it had with its last witness, the state called the Hunts' oldest daughter, Jo Ann, to testify, which drew an immediate objection from Thomas's attorneys. Judge Russell tested the six-year-old girl by allowing her to be questioned on the witness stand in the jury's absence by both sets of attorneys. When D.A. LaFont asked her the name of the man standing a few feet right of the witness stand, Jo Ann said with a soft voice and downcast reply, "that is Fred," indicating Dr. Fred Janes of Olton.

The scene of the petite Jo Ann sitting in the huge wooden witness chair was heartrending. Ruth Borchardt, Mae Hunt's sister, held Jo Ann's hand as attorneys from both sides plied her with questions. Jo Ann seemed most uneasy as she gazed toward her sister, Jane, who was in the arms of Dr. Alvin Borchardt, Mae's brother-in-law, but she did her best and answered the attorneys' questions.

The state rested its case after Judge Russell sustained the objections based on the contention that though intelligent for her age, Jo Ann was not old enough to comprehend the sanctity of testifying. The court ruled against her testimony's admissibility because Russell deemed her as an immature witness, even though she was the only person who saw the man who killed her parents. The state's paltry case was presented in a single day, going into the evening.

After the state rested, the defense team, including lead counsel Curtis Douglas of Panhandle, George McCarthy of Amarillo, and Charles Clements of Plainview requested a recess to talk with their client. They retired to an anteroom for about five minutes, and when they returned, Douglas announced to the court, "Your honor we have no witnesses. The defense rests."

The courtroom and hallways erupted with murmurings of disbelief like a prairie wildfire.

How could one of the most notorious murder cases in West Texas history go to trial without the defense offering any evidence or witnesses?

The murmurings grew noisier until the courtroom was a cacophony. Judge Russell banged his gavel repeatedly to bring the room back to order.

Once Douglas restored order, he promptly presented a motion for an instructed verdict of acquittal based on inadequate evidence. He also declared the chain of evidence did not coincide. Russell refused the motion. It took over two hours to prepare the court's charge for the jury.

On August 30, the case was sent to the jury of nine farmers and three automobile dealers at 5:00 p.m. For three and a half hours, jurors debated the case before assessing a guilty verdict and sentencing Thomas to death. When the verdict was read, an eerie silence filled the courtroom. Then, chaos erupted again. Thomas sat impassively at the defense table, as if deaf to the spectators' outbursts and the banging of Judge Russell's gavel. He brushed his chin with his right hand and swallowed but showed no other reaction.

For the first time since the trial started, Thomas was alone. His son Joe, brother Wilburn, and sister Opal had not reached the courtroom from the nearby Hilton Hotel a block away in time to hear the verdict.

Reporters scrambled toward Thomas, yelling questions. "Jim, do you have any statement?" one asked.

Thomas turned and said, "Yes—I'm not guilty. If I were guilty, I deserve it. But I am not guilty. A lot of things were never brought to the surface in this trial. I have the names of two persons who have not been before a grand jury. Convicting me won't solve the Hunt murder case. I don't know why someone couldn't find the witness on the subpoena list as Porter Humphries. I was baptized into the Christian church, and I never killed anyone. I have a reputation, but I never lived up to that reputation. I never killed anyone. Why should I be called a killer?"

Thomas's smile was long gone. His face was void of emotion and he continued talking to the reporters. One asked where he was on the night of the murders.

"I was out with a lady," he remarked with a nod of his head. "She is a married lady, and it wouldn't be chivalrous."

Another reporter asked, "Jim, you're reputed to have no fear, ever of anything have you ever felt fear?"

"Oh, many times, but I am not afraid."

"Jim, will you say a prayer for yourself tonight?"

With piercing eyes, Thomas replied, "I've already said it."

Before being transported back to the Lubbock County jail, Thomas stopped for a photographer who asked to take his photo. Thomas slyly said, "I've had my picture taken so many times." When the photographer explained it was for an assignment, Thomas grinned, nodded, and said, "Ok."

After returning to the jail, a few reporters continued to question him about his kids. Thomas leaned in on the bars and said, "I'm proud of them all, my boys and girls. When I served ten years in a Nebraska penitentiary, my younger boy thought I was working there, but when I got out, I called them into a huddle. I told them there was only one way to go, and I hadn't followed it."

Thomas's last words to reporters that evening, he said, "If I'm guilty, there's a way of proving it."

Jury Misconduct Revealed

A few days after Jim's trial ended, Judge Russell called a special hearing to determine if there had been jury misconduct.

The hearing on September 22, 1944, revealed that Thomas's criminal record had been mentioned during jury deliberations, which went against the charge to the jury. They were instructed that Thomas's past crimes could not be discussed or even considered during their deliberations.

Virgil Winn, the jury foreman, signed an affidavit stating there had been "some discussion and statements by some jurors that the defendant was an ex-convict. There was no discussion as to his record or what he had formerly been convicted of." Winn testified:

> While we were waiting for the charge of the court, Deputy Sheriff, Ted Andrews, took us for a walk in a part of town where we would not contact any crowds [sic]. As we were returning to the courthouse, one of the jurors saw some watermelons and wanted to purchase some from a sidewalk stand. As we were going into the jury room at the courthouse, Andrews handed one of the jurors a carton of Camel cigarettes and said they was given to the jury as compliments of the Plainview Chamber of Commerce [sic].
>
> A discussion began, we talked about how the defendant failed to put on any witnesses and I thought the jury was about to get into the discussion the defendant failed to testify and I immediately told the jury they could not discuss it because the court had told us not to. There was some discussion and statements to the fact by some of the jurors the defendant was an ex-convict but there was no discussion as to his record or what he had formerly been convicted of.

Juror J.M. Stubblefield also testified that a discussion among some jurors included a mention that Thomas was an ex-convict, and another juror remarked, "How come him out of the penitentiary?" Juror Elgar Winn said that jurors discussed Thomas's record after the jury was impaneled, but not after the jury was charged or during deliberations.

After the hearing, the defense filed a motion for a new trial. The six-page document listed more than a dozen points of contention, including that the defendant went to trial without a material witness: Porter Humphries.

On October 5, 1944, Russell ordered the verdict set aside and granted Thomas receive a new trial.

A few days later, Thomas's attorneys requested another venue change, arguing their client could not get a fair trial in Hale County, and Russell granted the application. The case was moved to Lamesa in Dawson County, more than a hundred miles south of Plainview.

Thomas's Second Trial in Dawson County

A few weeks later, a preliminary hearing was scheduled for the new trial in Lamesa, but Judge Louis Reed failed to appear for court in mid-October. No reason given for his absence, but it meant a new judge had to be chosen for Thomas's case.

In rural country style, Dawson County Sheriff Buck Bennett stood on the north side courthouse steps and instructed the eight lawyers assembled to elect a special judge of the court. These lawyers were a mix of men serving the state and in private practice. They were Karl Clayton, Joseph Garland, Rollen McCord, Kilmer Corbin, Carl Rountree, Valdimer Key, Bob Huff, and Emmet Warren.

They elected Joseph Garland on October 16, 1944. Garland then set Thomas's second trial for three months later, on January 8, 1945. On January 3, Thomas was transported from the Lubbock County Jail to the Lamesa courthouse, where he immediately entered a not guilty plea. Eighty prospective jurors were called for this trial.

As in Plainview, a huge crowd congregated in the small town of Lamesa. Hotel rooms were reserved in advance, leaving only private homes to rent. The small second-story courtroom, covered in oak from floor to ceiling, was packed with three hundred to four hundred visitors. Before the trial began, defense attorney Kilmer Corbin told reporters that "Jim seemed to be in the best of spirits."

This trial opened on a Monday, and jury selection lasted into the night. Ten lawyers participated in this trial: five for the state and five for the defense. Prosecutors called thirty witnesses, while the defense subpoenaed only six.

Defense attorney John McNamara, during cross-examination, got Ewell Hunt to state that Billy Newton had been convicted of attempting to take Roy Hunt's life. Investigator Aubrey Fawver, Sherriff Hutson, as well as Ewell, all testified on the conditions of the Hunts' bodies, chronicling in detail how they were bound.

The Hunts' oldest daughter, Jo Ann, was called again as a witness. She was escorted into this oak courtroom by her aunt, Ruth Borchardt. As her questioning began, she broke down crying and was led from the courtroom. After she returned with her tears dried but eyes still red, Judge Garland asked her if anyone had been in her home the night her father and mother died. Jo Ann answered, "A big man was there." Garland ruled her competent to testify after she replied, "I'd get punished if I didn't tell the truth," which generated smiles from the courtroom audience.

Fitfully twisting a tiny handkerchief between her small hands and sobbing, the seven-year-old told the hushed courtroom her version of what she remembered. Ruth stood by the witness stand and held Jo Ann's hand as she answered questions. Judge Garland again asked Jo Ann if there had been anyone in her home the night her parents died. "Yes, sir," she said, wiping her reddened eyes. "A big man was there, and he had on black shoes." Sadly, she could give no other description in the tense quiet courtroom. "He put me in a closet and shut the door." Tears rolled down the cheeks of two jury members as Jo Ann finished her testimony. Thomas remained emotionless during her time in court.

Several witnesses from the Hale County trial could not testify at this trial because they were ill or had moved away because of marriage, new jobs, or military service. The chief eyewitness who saw Thomas in Littlefield, Eddie Glass, had moved to Clovis, New Mexico.

Nineteen state exhibits were admitted during this trial. Expert witnesses with the Texas DPS testified mainly to the evidence of the automobile tracks, casts of footprints, tennis shoes, and string pieces.

The defense did not cross-examine any of the state's witnesses, except for Ewell. When prosecutors rested, defense attorney Curtis Douglas—who also represented Thomas in the Plainview trial—rose and proclaimed, "Your honor, we have no witnesses."

Testimony had begun on a Tuesday, and on Thursday, the two sides took about four hours for their closing arguments, beginning at 3:00 p.m. The case went to the jury at midnight, and by noon, they rendered a guilty verdict and sentenced Thomas to death.

Thomas, standing to receive the verdict, was unresponsive as each juror was polled for their verdict. Prosecutors had once again relied on circumstantial evidence to convince a jury to convict Thomas.

Historical photo of Dawson County Courthouse.
Christena Stephens

NO. 2803.

THE STATE OF TEXAS	)	IN THE DISTRICT COURT
VS.	)	OF
JIM THOMAS	)	HALE COUNTY, TEXAS.

VERDICT OF THE JURY

We the jury find the defendant *GUILTY*

AND ASSESS PUNISHMENT OF DEATH PENALTY

Foreman.

The jury verdict sentencing Jim Thomas to death in Hale County.
Christena Stephens

INSUFFICIENT EVIDENCE

Thomas's attorneys, in an appeal filed on May 8, 1945, challenged all the evidence in the Dawson County case, claiming it was insufficient to warrant a conviction.

Six months later, the appeals court rendered its opinion, with Judge Lloyd Davidson summarizing the case. The conclusions centered on the evidence of the tire tracks and tennis shoes.

Davidson noted that Thomas did not testify on his own behalf. He also commented on the inconsistencies in the prosecution's case. Investigators found no fingerprints or other evidence at the house that could identify the murderer, and nothing in the house appeared to have been missing or stolen.

He noted that if the fatal bullet was recovered, it was not introduced during the trial, and no testimony specified the bullet's caliber. And he said there was no indication of blood on the bed or Roy Hunt's clothing and most importantly, nothing reflected if Jim was arrested or taken into custody.

As to the tennis shoes, he said that Thomas had visited the Veazey home and Veazey's garage had an electric tire machine with an attached steel wire buffing brush and an Emory wheel, which were used to roughen the surface of automobile inner tubes when making repairs. And Thomas had access to the garage because the Veazey's kept a key to it on a nail inside their home.

The footprints formed the crux of the State's case. The Veazey's seventeen-year-old son, Alvis, played high school basketball and wore rubber-soled tennis shoes. Alvis identified the shoes in question as his own and testified that the last time he had seen the shoes was Friday afternoon before the murders. Alvis even asserted that the buffed places on the tennis shoes were not there when he had last seen them. He was present when officers had taken the shoes from his closet but had not noticed the buffed places at that time. But the shoe tracks at the crime scene had three raised places or bars in the plaster cast that did not match the soles of Alvis Veazey's tennis shoes presented in court.

Davidson found that unless the tracks at the crime scene were made by the Veazey tennis shoes, the state's case failed to identify Thomas as the murderer. But Alvis Veazey's tennis shoes were a common type, character, and design. Based on measurements at the crime scene, the footprints were made by a size ten tennis shoe, but the size of the tennis shoes introduced into evidence was never indicated.

Even if the tracks had been made by Veazey's shoes, prosecutors never established that Thomas wore them. What's more, prosecutors never introduced testimony about Thomas's shoe size, even though he'd been in state custody for months.

This also applies to the tire tracks. Nothing indicates that the tire tracks at the crime scene were made exclusively by the Lee tire on the Craig automobile. In addition, Davidson took issue with prosecutors' claims that the right front tire on the Craig automobile that Jim had borrowed had been switched before and after the murders.

Davidson also took issue with the state's reliance on the pieces of string, one of which was found on the comforter covering the Hunts' bodies and the other found in the Veazey's garage.

The Judge proceeded in summarizing the witness statements about Jim being in Amarillo and Littlefield, as well as borrowing both the Veazey and Craig cars. He continued by indicating that late Tuesday afternoon, Jim asked Craig to drive him to Childress. They arrived at about 9:30 p.m. Between 10:30 and 11:00 p.m. Tuesday night, Thomas called Marie Hall of Galveston, and she told him the Galveston County sheriff was looking for him. But she didn't testify where he was calling from.

Davidson noted that the state's evidence showed that at 10:30 p.m. on the night of murders someone giving the name of Wilson called Marie from Vernon to Galveston, with the call ended at about midnight. Thomas's last-known whereabouts were in Childress at 9:30 p.m. where Craig left him, more than 150 miles from the Hunts' home.

While he found that Thomas may have been in Littlefield the night of the murders and could have committed the murders, the same could be said of all Littlefield residents. Showing that someone has the opportunity to commit a crime is not sufficient to prove that they did. What's more, the only eyewitness, Jo Ann Hunt, did not identify Thomas as the man she saw in her home.

As a result, Davidson ruled that the evidence was insufficient to warrant a murder conviction. He noted that under Texas law, to convict someone with circumstantial evidence the facts must show guilt and exclude every other reasonable hypothesis.

"Proof amounting to a strong suspicion or probability is not sufficient to support any conviction," he wrote. "Even having the opportunity or being in a position to commit a crime does not constitute proof that a crime was committed by that person."

He noted that the identity of the accused committing the alleged crime depended on tracks or footprints, and the evidence must be convincing and leave no reasonable doubt.

Davidson took issue with the state's reliance on the pieces of string, one found on the comforter covering the Hunts' bodies and another found in the Veazey's Garage.

He analyzed everything in the appeal by rhetorically asking, "Do all the facts and evidence warrant and justify the State's contention?

By considering the facts in light of the aforementioned rules, Jim was in Littlefield the night of the murders and was in a position to have committed the murders. However, such an act is likewise true of all other inhabitants of Littlefield."

He continued by saying the state placed Jim at the scene of the crime to establish their assurances on the footprints and automobile tracks. And, most importantly, Jo Ann made no effort to identify Thomas as the man she saw in her home.

He argued that the appeals court searched the record for any testimony showing the size of the shoe worn by Thomas to see if he was even capable of wearing the Veazey shoes. With Thomas under arrest and in custody, the state should have obtained a pair of his shoes or at least determined his shoe size.

This also applies to the tire tracks. Nothing indicates that the tire tracks at the crime scene were made exclusively by the Lee tire on the Craig automobile.

Davidson stated, "In this land of ours, we know the life and liberty of no man shall be exacted or taken from him as a penalty for the crime until his guilt has been first established in accordance with law, it is the right guaranteed every citizen."

He concluded by saying, "it is the duty and responsibility of the courts to enforce and preserve that right. In the performance of duty and in all consciousness of that responsibility, the evidence is insufficient to authorize the conviction."

With this final comment, Davidson reversed Thomas's conviction on October 3, 1945.

ONE MORE TIME

After the Dawson County reversal, the Hunt family retreated from the public eye to deal with the shock of the appeals court's decision.

For Harold LaFont, the reversal was a brutal professional blow. Several weeks passed before he began pursuing a new trial for Thomas. He was doing it with nearly the identical evidence presented at the Dawson County trial. In his correspondence with Dawson County Judge Louis Reed both agreed that they should move the trial to Sweetwater in Nolan County, about a hundred miles away.

Reed wrote to Judge Albert Mauzey expressing concern about seating a jury in Lamesa or the surrounding counties because of the publicity. Mauzey accepted Thomas's case, and Reed transferred it to Nolan County in August 1946.

Trying Thomas became more challenging because witnesses were becoming less cooperative. They were tired of the drawn-out case, and many were belligerent toward LaFont and the court system.

In September 1946, LaFont wrote to Nolan County defense attorney Charles Dunn, saying several of the state's witnesses were scattered across Texas and other states, and they would need to be re-subpoenaed to testify. In closing, he remarked, "I think you will find this quite an interesting case."

LaFont wrote to Sheriff Hutson in early October 1946, requesting that Hutson ensure Roy Granbery and Pearl Stokes be in Sweetwater. Stokes, who had not testified in the previous trials, was an eyewitness from the Stokes Drugstore in Littlefield. Late in the investigation, she said she saw Thomas near her husband's drugstore on the Sunday night before the murders.

Stokes insisted she did not want to go to Sweetwater to identify Thomas. When Hutson relayed her response to LaFont, the D.A. became furious and yelled, "If not voluntarily, I will subpoena her. We need to make sure Jim was the man she saw." LaFont never followed through on his threat.

Following routine protocol in the mid-1940s, Thomas was transferred from the Lubbock County Jail to the Nolan County Jail two weeks before the trial.

On the placid, chilly morning of Tuesday, October 15, 1946, Thomas's third trial for Roy's murder opened in the 32nd District Court in Sweetwater, a town of about ten thousand people aptly named for its sweet-tasting water.

A special venire of 144 men was summoned. Sitting this jury proved tedious, and by the end of the first day, only two had been selected. The state's questions included asking if potential jurors had objections to the death penalty.

Other questions to these potential jurors dealt with family, religious convictions, and knowledge of previous prosecutions. They were also asked if they had read newspaper accounts of the former trials, or if they had spoken to any witnesses. The final jury comprised a shoe salesman, oil refinery workers, farmers, a shop foreman, a groceryman, and a cabinet shop employee.

With the jury seated by late Wednesday, testimony began on Thursday morning. Defense attorney Nunn assisted the prosecution, along with George Outlaw from Sweetwater, George Dupree from Lubbock, and of course, Harold LaFont.

Twenty-seven state witnesses and five defense witnesses had arrived in the town named for its water. Thomas's lead attorney, John McNamara of Waco, was an older criminal lawyer who built his reputation on protecting his clients. He had also served as the former McLennan County Attorney.

The sensationalism of this case had not waned for spectators. They still had questions and wanted answers. As the proceedings began, the courtroom once again became packed, with spectators spilling into the hallway beyond. Anticipating some long days, most brought their lunches to avoid losing their coveted courtroom seats. Thomas's brother, Wilburn, and his sister, Opal, were in court, but no one from the Hunt or Frank families.

The first witness to take the stand was Roy Granbery, who described the location and structure of the Hunt home. Granbery, an abstractor, was one of the three people who last saw the Hunts alive. Both Sherriff Hutson and Lubbock Police Department Identification Officer Aubrey Fawver gave in-depth details on the location of the Hunt's home and the condition of the bedroom, as well as the bed on which the bodies were found. Furthermore, they each specified as to the position and condition of their bodies and particular articles collected as evidence.

Fawver's testimony was almost a mirror image of what he gave at the Dawson trial regarding the location of the footprints. He explained that the prints were deeper on the right inside track. He then testified on the tire tracks and said they were found one block from the Hunt home. They were similar to a track made by one of the tires on the Craig car, which Thomas had allegedly borrowed. The jury heard Texas Ranger Norvell Redwine recap the condition of the Hunt bodies.

Mayda Grissom, whom the Hunt girls ran to after leaving their home, sobbed throughout her testimony regarding the angst of the daughters. She recounted how she carried Jane back into the Hunt home, but Jo Ann refused to go back inside with her.

For the first time, Dr. Fred Janes testified that he examined Roy's body in the funeral home and removed the fatal bullet. He described the bullet wound and stated that it had been "almost directly between the eyes, and the bullet almost went straight back, almost directly straight into Roy's skull."

George Gambill, a state firearm and identification expert, at the time of the investigation, testified he examined the shoes and plaster cast, and LaFont asked him to point out to the jury any conclusions he had drawn from his examination. Gambill pointed to certain spots on the shoes' insteps, saying they had been buffed.

Upon his cross-examination, Gambill stated that the shoes were altered after the prints were made and that the shoes, as entered into evidence, could not have made the tracks in question. Defense attorney Charles Farmer asked him, "is this particular pair of shoes the only pair the manufacturer had made?" He replied, "I should not think so." Farmer declared during Gambill's questioning that the shoe marks on the instep could have been caused by resting the foot on a rough object.

Thomas once again remained composed during the trial. His brother and sister were always close by. He grinned frequently and always appeared in court as a well-dressed businessman in a blue pinstripe suit and a blue tie printed with small white polka dots.

In this third trial, the state presented twenty-three exhibits, including five black and white crime scene photographs, two of which showed the Hunt bodies and a third presenting a scene outside the house. The defense firmly objected to these crime scene photos, saying they would incite the jury.

The jury also examined pieces of rope removed from both bodies, the string taken from the foot of the bed, and wire removed from Roy's wrists and from around Mae's left arm. Glen McLaughlin testified extensively as to the two pieces of string.

Levi Duncan testified that the Craig car was in the alley and that it had struck and smashed a solid object, such as a rock. The prosecution produced two pictures of the car and the rock. Duncan also said one of the car's tires showed evidence of having hit a solid object like a rock.

The former Irene Craig, who was now Irene Hnulik, nervously testified that before Thomas borrowed her car, she had damaged it on one of the curbs at the Amarillo Post Office. She said that Ranger Gault did not believe her story of her damaging the car herself. No officers ever interviewed her, except when she was called to Amarillo Sheriff Bill Adam's office. She said LaFont threatened her with perjury before her testimony in anteroom outside the court. She was adamant that she told LaFont about the damage at the grand jury in Olton, but he never called her to testify as a witness in the previous trials. She screeched back at him, "Harold, I don't like to be threatened." In response she said, LaFont calmly boasted, "Mrs. Hnulik I am not threatening you. I will send you to the penitentiary for perjury." Nothing ever came from that heated exchange.

Ranger Gault testified that he had known Thomas since 1929. This time, Gault testified that Thomas wore a size eight-and-a-half shoe in October 1943. He also said he took the shoes to Alvis Veazey, who was stationed at an Arkansas Army camp, to have him identify them.

The court reporter then re-read the question-and-answer testimony given by Eddie Glass, the Littlefield café owner. Glass was now in California. The State offered the defense an opportunity to cross-examine Glass by the same method.

Fawver took the stand once again to identify the car photos that he took on November 6, 1943. When the defense questioned him, he stated that to his knowledge, it was the first time the pictures were entered as evidence.

The state's last witness was Jo Ann, now eight years old. No tears stained her cheeks this time as she stoically walked down the center of the courtroom. Taking a seat in the big wooden oak chair, she testified that she went into her parents' bedroom when the killer was in the room.

"A big man, wearing black shoes, was in there and he picked me up and put me in the closet," she answered in an unsure voice.

During her testimony, she was never questioned about which closet she had been placed in. Everyone assumed it was the nursery closet. Nor was she questioned on the witness stand about how she and Jane had left the house. When asked if she saw her parents' bodies, she responded, "I didn't look." Then, taking in gulps of air and trying to keep calm, Jo Ann's cheeks reddened, and she burst into tears, covering her face with her hands. She was led from the courtroom, her loud sobs filling the hallway.

At no time did the defense put its own witnesses on the stand and recalled only five of the state's. The prosecution rested at about 2:00 p.m. on Friday.

The jury received the case after midnight because the court went into the night to hear the lengthy closing arguments. The jury returned a guilty verdict and sentenced Thomas to life in prison at 3:20 p.m. on Saturday, October 19.

Considering the trial's outcome, Thomas appeared jovial. Escorted into Judge Mauzey's chambers, he signed several papers without reading them. A court official asked him, "Aren't you afraid you'll be charged with perjury by signing papers you haven't read?" Thomas replied with a chuckle, "I don't see how I could; I'm in deep enough trouble as is."

Mauzey assessed Thomas's sentence to ninety-nine years in prison. Asked if he had anything to say after the sentence was pronounced, Thomas turned his eyes towards the courtroom window as the day was growing colder and barely shook his head no.

Thomas was remanded to the Nolan County Jail, and the sheriff was ordered to deliver him to the state prison in Huntsville.

His gentlemanly good humor changed to acrimony once he was back behind the cell bars, where a reporter tried asking him some questions. Thomas slammed against the bars and cursed at the reporter, saying, "If I could get out of this cell, I'd beat the hell out of you. I don't owe that goddammed newspaper nothing." His curses were unrelenting until a deputy quieted him down.

Almost a month later, on November 16, in the Nolan County courtroom, Thomas's lawyers called for a motion to set aside the jury verdict and requested a new trial. The motion argued, among other things, that the court erred in admitting insufficient evidence to support the verdict and that the Grissoms' testimonies were hearsay and immaterial. The defense also said that chemist Glen McLaughlin's testimony about the two pieces of string, delivered in front of the jury box rather than from the witness stand, was unprecedented.

Judge Mauzey rejected the motion, and Thomas's lawyers promptly gave notice of appeal. They were granted sixty days, the time allowed by Texas law to prepare and file bills of exceptions.

Nolan County Courthouse.
Sweetwater County Historical Museum

When Governor,

COKE STEVENSON
PAROLED
JIM THOMAS!

At the time **JIM THOMAS** was **PAROLED BY COKE STEVEN-SON**, Thomas was serving a prison term for assault with attempt to murder Baxter Honey, respected Lubbock citizen and longtime peace officer. In addition, Thomas had a long criminal record in Texas and in Nebraska.

"This was done without any notification of any of the local authorities connected with his trial."

After **JIM THOMAS WAS PAROLED BY COKE STEVENSON,** he was **THRICE TRIED AND THRICE CONVICTED OF COMPLICITY IN THE MURDERS OF DR. AND MRS. ROY HUNT** in Littlefield. West Texans, remember on Saturday:

COKE STEVENSON
PAROLED
JIM THOMAS!

(This advertisement paid for by Burton S. Burks (District Attorney at that time) and other citizens of Lubbock county.)

A newspaper ad criticizing Gov. Coke Stevenson for paroling Jim Thomas.
Newspaper Archive

FAILING A THIRD TIME

Thomas's lawyers filed for an extension on December 12, 1946, to continue preparing the statement of facts in their client's second appeal. Thomas, meanwhile, awaited the outcome in the Nolan County Jail.

By February 1947, D.A. LaFont wrote letters to the Texas attorney general and George Outlaw, another attorney, who helped try Thomas's third trial. The letters conveyed LaFont's sense of exhaustion. He was worn out by the Hunt case and did not want to spend any more time or money on it.

His letters stated how he wanted off the case, and he suggested that someone else should argue Thomas's case before the Court of Criminal Appeals. He wanted a dismissal from the case.

"It should be argued and briefed...but not by me." LaFont offered his cooperation, including going to Austin, but he stated that the Hunt family should pay the attorney's expenses for the appeal. He claimed he had already spent his own money prosecuting the case, and he did not relish the expense of another trip to Austin. If he had to argue this appeal, and the Hunts would not pay, he wanted reimbursement from the state.

The AG's office responded that under the law, an active district attorney could not claim expenses while appearing before the appeals court. The prosecuting attorney had a duty to represent the state in all proceedings before the court.

LaFont was livid, and it did not help that he had received a phone call from Ewell Hunt pleading with him to argue Thomas's appeal.

In letters to Outlaw and D.A. Nunn in April 1947, both of whom had helped prosecute the Nolan trial, his attitude changed, and he agreed to argue this appeal in Austin. LaFont asked the Nolan County judge to send the state's exhibits to Austin. LaFont half-heartedly reiterated his plan to work on this case. In closing, he stated they should go ahead and file a brief because Ewell Hunt had paid for the Sweetwater trial Statement of Facts at twenty cents per page.

In May 1947, attorneys from both sides appeared in Austin to present their arguments. Defense attorney Curtis Douglas, who had made a career out of defending Thomas, helped argue the appeal.

Like all the other appeals involving the Newton and Thomas cases, this one was heard inside the Texas Capitol, in the Court of Appeals Chamber. The small chamber was set up much like a standard courtroom. Three judges' chairs were positioned on a bench at the front, the witness box was to their right, and a long attorney table was in the middle of the chamber. Instead of traditional bench seating for attendees, wooden armchairs were placed in rows.

The appeals court heard the defense's arguments first. The state presented new evidence, including damage to the fender of the Craig's car, but it did not strengthen the prosecutors' argument, and the circumstantial evidence still did not exclude other hypotheses. The defense contended the new evidence was not sufficient to link Thomas to the crime and that his size eight-and-a-half-inch foot proved only that he could have worn the ten-and-a-half-inch tennis shoes.

The defense maintained that no motive had been shown for Thomas to murder the Hunts and that at none of Thomas's trials had the state shown that Billy Newton had been investigated for the murder.

LaFont argued that prosecutors at this Sweetwater trial had shown that Thomas could wear the tennis shoes found in the Veazey home and that similar shoes had made the tracks around the Hunt home.

He also contended that the state's case was stronger this time because of the evidence of the damaged car that Thomas had borrowed, including the discovery of black marks on a piece of concrete two hundred feet from the Hunt home.

He said the tire tracks behind the home showed a certain tire type was used on the left front wheel of the car. The car Thomas borrowed had a similar tire on its right front wheel.

LaFont explained that Eva Veazey, in whose home Thomas stayed, said Thomas was the only man who had access to the shoes and the garage. Appeals Court Judge Tom Beauchamp interrupted LaFont to ask if a woman could have had access to the shoes, and LaFont replied yes.

The arguments took an entire day at the Texas Capital, and it would be almost two months before the court made its ruling. After LaFont returned to Plainview, he wrote to Ewell, saying he felt the court would grant the appeal. In closing, he noted that he had spent $67.70 going to Austin for the hearing and he would appreciate Ewell sending reimbursement.

After scrutinizing every word of the trial record regarding the appeal arguments, the appeals court came back with its opinion on June 28, 1947. Judge Charles Krueger noted that no one testified that Thomas knew the location of the Hunt home, let alone the layout of the house. Yes, Thomas violated parole by going to Amarillo to visit Sid Veazey, but the state presented no evidence that Thomas knew Roy Hunt. The record was silent on why the sheriff was looking for him.

As for the tire tracks in the alley behind the Hunts' home, they indicated a Lee tire on the left front wheel had been in the alley. The Craig automobile, which Thomas borrowed, had a Lee tire on the right front wheel. Unless the Lee tire on the Craig car was changed from the left to the right after leaving the alley, it was not the Craig car that had been in the alley.

The state's new evidence involved damage to the running boards of the Craig car, which prosecutors contended was caused by a cement block in the alley that was damaged, perhaps by being backed over by an automobile. However, Mrs. Craig testified that she had run into a curb while parking in Amarillo before Thomas borrowed the car, a detail she shared with the officers who inspected the car when they came to talk to her. She even showed them the spot at the post office where this occurred. She also testified that one of the prosecuting attorneys, and another person wearing a blue suit, took her into the private chamber of the presiding judge, a few minutes prior to the time she took the witness stand, and said they would prosecute her for perjury if she testified to doing the damage to the car herself.

Prosecutors also failed to connect the two-inch piece of string found on the oil drum stove in the Veazey's garage, one hundred twenty miles north of Littlefield, to a similar one found on the Hunts' bed. They could not establish who placed the string on the stove or how long it had been there is left to conjecture. The prosecution's expert witness could not swear that it was a piece from the same string from the bed. The jury cannot be more certain than the witness in determining if the evidence measures up to convicting the defendant.

Kruger found that Thomas's connection with the horrible crime depended entirely on circumstantial evidence, and that to warrant a conviction, each fact had to be proved by competent evidence beyond a reasonable doubt. The facts must be consistent with each other. It's not sufficient the circumstances coincide with the account, and therefore render probable the guilt of the defendant; they must exclude every other reasonable hypothesis except of the defendant's guilt, and unless they do so beyond a reasonable doubt, the evidence is not sufficient to warrant a conviction.

Now let us analyze the circumstances proved in this case to determine whether they meet the requirements of the law. The fact that Thomas was in Littlefield on the night of October 25, several hours before the murders, is of little value without other circumstances that connect him with this crime. The fact that human tracks were found near the Hunts' house, and that they were made with size ten-and-a-half shoes, would not implicate Thomas unless prosecutors could show that he had such shoes and that those particular shoes made the tracks.

The size ten-and-a-half shoes connecting Jim to the tracks were the same pair that Jim had access to at the Veazey's. These shoes were taken by the officers and were presented to Mr. Veazey's son for identification. He examined them closely with the purpose of identifying them as his shoes, which he did. No particular marks or abrasions on the shoes were called to his attention at the time, nor did he notice any early in the investigation. Later, the shoes were taken by a Texas Ranger to Arkadelphia, Arkansas, where the shoes were again shown to him. What appeared to be certain marks or abrasions were pointed out to him and it was then, for the first time, he noticed them. Who made the marks and abrasions, and how long they had been on the shoes, remains unanswered.

If the shoes were in the condition on the night in question, they could not have made the tracks found at the Hunt home. The state needed to prove the shoes were not in the scuffed condition at the time of the murders. The state tried to explain this by showing there was a buffing machine and a wire brush in the Veazey garage to which Thomas had access, arguing that he buffed the shoes after the murders and returned them to the closet. In other words, the prosecution presumed that he wore shoes that were too big, and then presumed he scuffed them before returning them. Rules of evidence, however, prohibit basing one presumption on another. As a result, the evidence was insufficient to sustain the conviction.

For the third time, the state failed to convict Thomas of Roy Hunt's murder.

The Court of Appeals, which at the time was in state Capitol in Austin.
Texas Supreme Court

IT'S OVER

Because of the trials and appeals, Thomas had been in jail since October 1943, and by the time of the final appeals court decision, he had served his five-year sentence for the Baxter Honey assault. He walked out of the Nolan County Jail as a free man and tipped his hat to reporters, telling them he was going on an extended fishing trip. He entered a car and drove east towards Fort Worth.

With Thomas cleared in the case and no other suspects identified, the Hunt and Frank families were left with no answers and no justice.

What became of Thomas?

His life became almost conventional. He purchased a house in Fort Worth's Arlington Heights neighborhood in 1948 for $2,500. He lived there with his wife, Mary, and worked in an Odessa nightclub and a Waco drug store.

Thomas may have settled down in one of Fort Worth's nicest neighborhoods, but his troubles with the law did not stop.

In the summer of 1947, not long after his release from Nolan County, police questioned Thomas in various murder investigations, including cases involving known gamblers in the Dallas and Fort

Worth areas. Every time he was detained for questioning, Thomas's name appeared yet again in the newspapers, with the stories noting his ties to the Hunt murders. Each time he was questioned, however, he was released and never charged. Nonetheless, many Texas newspapers referred to him as one of Fort Worth's leading underworld characters.

In March 1948, police questioned Thomas about Lon Holley's death. Holley, a Fort Worth café and liquor store owner, was in his car when he was shot twice in the back of his head on March 7, 1948.

Almost immediately, investigators picked up Thomas in downtown Fort Worth. After answering the phone on the night of his death, Holley had scribbled "Jim Thomas" and "Frank Cates" on a scratch pad. He later told his wife, "If I don't get home by midnight, you'll know something has happened to me."

Thomas was in an agreeable mood when he arrived at police head-quarters in downtown Fort Worth. Always dapper, reporters noted he wore a tan sports coat, a dark brown sports shirt, brown slacks, and a flower tie. He told police he didn't shoot Holley.

"I wouldn't shoot anybody. Why, human life is a flowering bud to me. I wouldn't crush it," Thomas quipped.

Now a soft-spoken, complacent man, he was released after two hours of questioning.

Officers theorized Holley was murdered because he knew too much about other crimes, including a recent $16,000 bank robbery in Rosebud, Texas, where a night watchman was bound and gagged at gunpoint while two men robbed the bank.

But Holley also had a connection to the Hunt murders.

He had turned over a .38-caliber revolver to Fort Worth detectives purportedly claiming it as the Hunt murder weapon. The gun was examined, but ballistics tests were never made public. Police revealed only that they could not definitively identify the gun as the one that had killed Roy. All detectives said about this gun was it was a new handgun.

A few months later, Thomas was questioned in the murder of Que R. Miller, the former sheriff of Foard County, Texas, who was convicted of misappropriation of public funds. Miller was found dead in a car in Oakland Park in October 1948, with a gunshot to the back of the head. In December 1950, police questioned Thomas about the nitroglycerin car bombing deaths of gambler Nelson Harris and his pregnant wife, Juanita, a month earlier.

Less than a year later, Thomas was questioned in the death of Herbert Noble, a Dallas gambler and nightclub owner. Noble was also known as "The Cat," and "Human Clay Pigeon." Twelve previous attempts on Noble's life had failed, although his wife, Mildred, had been killed two years earlier by a car bomb. On August 8, 1951, the thirteenth attempt came in the form of a land mine placed near Noble's mailbox. The blast left a six-foot-wide, three-foot-deep hole where Noble had been standing.

What Thomas Did Not See Coming

On a sweltering, humid Wednesday in August 1951, Thomas ate breakfast, kissed Mary goodbye, and started his 1950 Ford F6 truck, which he had purchased a few days before from his friend Hubert Deere in Oklahoma.

Only Jim knew what was going on in his mind as he drove 120 miles to Durant, Oklahoma, where he planned to confront Deere, a friend of ten years, for misrepresenting the condition of the two-ton truck. Thomas complained the truck's battery was bad, among other faults.

Their friendship started in movie-scene style in 1941, when their cars collided on West Sixth Street in Amarillo. Deere sustained a knee injury. From then on, they were involved in business and social activities, and Deere borrowed money from Thomas several times.

They were both arrested in late 1941 in Texarkana, Texas, in connection with a bank robbery in Mexia. Deere, who was held for three hours and released, said, "I just made the mistake of being with Jim Thomas."

As Thomas left the main highway from Fort Worth, he turned toward Durant's downtown area. After driving around downtown, he found Deere standing on a corner.

Thomas parked his truck and sauntered over to Deere, who was talking to another friend. Thomas plucked at Deere's rear pocket, brazenly interrupting the conversation by saying, "You told me a lie about that truck, and I think you told me a lie about that drill!"

Deere was thirty-nine years old, with blue eyes, sandy hair, and a stocky build. He spoke with a slight speech impediment.

Thomas started grumbling aloud on the street that the truck had a bad battery, and that it had cost him forty dollars to fix the broken windshield, instead of the twenty- or twenty-five-dollars Deere said it would cost. As he ran through his list of perceived slights, Thomas's voice grew louder. He started yelling obscenities, accusing Deere of stealing a drill. Deere shouted back, saying that he had returned the drill to his Midland tourist camp at least two or three months ago.

The fifty-six-year-old Thomas, who now weighed well over two hundred pounds, continued berating and cursing at Deere on the street corner.

"I think the goddamn drill is in your house," he yelled. "I'm gonna come down, pick up those damn truck sideboards, and look for it. I'm coming out to your house, and if it's not there I'm going to beat your damn head off."

Their public confrontation ended when Deere turned away from Thomas and walked three blocks west to his modest rented white cottage. The little house was organized and spotless. Deere lived alone while his family was in Amarillo.

He knew Thomas well, and he knew Thomas would make good on his threat. When he arrived at his house, Deere grabbed his twelve-gauge, double-barrel shotgun, loaded it with buckshot, and leaned it against a dining room wall. Then he sat down and waited. Tired of waiting for Thomas, he rose and started preparing his lunch. Then, at about noon, Thomas pulled up in front of the house.

"While I was at home prepping my lunch, I heard the truck drive up and stop and saw Thomas getting out the truck," Deere stated. "I met him at the door and told him, 'If you're still mad and crazy don't come in.' He slapped me across the mouth and pushed his way in. As Jim stepped in, I said, 'Don't start any trouble here or I'll kill you.'"

In seconds, he grabbed the loaded shotgun and pulled the trigger, firing both barrels at Thomas, who dropped dead on the floor.

No one witnessed the shooting, but Jack Walton, the courthouse custodian who was home for lunch had heard the shots.

Minutes after he regained his composure, Deere ambled out his back door, laid the shotgun on the porch, and walked three blocks east to the fire department to call an ambulance. He quietly strolled up to the police chief, who was nearby, said he had shot a man and surrendered.

The sheriff and deputies entered Deere's house cautiously and found Thomas lying on his stomach between the living room and the dining room.

Sheriff Bill Barker bent down and examined Thomas's back for wounds, then turned the body over, revealing two bullet wounds, as well as powder burns, indicating Deere had fired at close range. One blast caught Thomas in the upper stomach. The other tore through his groin, piercing his billfold in his right hip pocket. He had died instantly. No weapons were found on him—only a small pocketknife in his left pants pocket.

Sitting in a wooden chair in front of a window at the City Jail, Deere was uncuffed. He was surrounded by deputies as he recounted the events several times. He said Thomas had accused him of stealing a drill and complained about the problems with the truck.

"I was scared so bad," he told the deputies. "I killed Jim Thomas, but it certainly was self-defense." Declining to disparage Jim, Hubert continued, "Jim was a friend of mine. I have seen him many times since meeting him ten years ago and have borrowed money from him on several occasions. We even had an argument last year over a few gallons of paint."

But Deere added that he was wary of his friend's temper.

"I was afraid of him. It started with a cuss fight and developed to the point of kill or be killed. I sure regret killing him. I warned him to stay away from me. He drove up in front of my place and started up. I met him at the door and told him to stay out. He pulled open the door and slapped me in the mouth. I went into the dining room and got the gun, and he followed me. I told him to quit coming in. He kept coming, and I shot him."

Deere told the deputies that Thomas said he had been framed for the Hunt murders. "He said he was innocent, and I believed him."

In the early evening hours, Thomas's twenty-five-year-old wife, Mary, arrived to claim his body and personal effects, including $220 in cash. Her father, Paul Burton of Fort Worth, and Thomas's daughter, Adele Thomas Coble, accompanied her.

R.H. Mills, the district attorney of Bryan County, Oklahoma, questioned Mary for over an hour.

"I'm shocked and can't understand the shooting and don't have any idea what it was about," she said while dabbing tears from her eyes.

A photo of Thomas's corpse, lying in a Durant funeral home, was published as front-page news in the *Durant Weekly News*. His body was transported to Waco, the town where he had been a city fireman, painter, and bootlegger.

He was buried the next day in the historic Oakwood Cemetery in Waco under an oak tree in the Thomas family plot. His funeral services were cloaked in secrecy, with only family members attending.

Justice and Deere

Deere was charged with Jim's murder on September 29, 1951. He pleaded not guilty.

Sheriff Barker was convinced Deere knew more than he was telling.

He commented, "It doesn't seem likely a man like Jim Thomas would drive to Durant from Fort Worth to argue over an electric drill. We may never know the true story behind the slaying, but we aren't accepting his version as the complete truth until we completely check it out."

Deere's trial began in November 1951, and Judge Sam Sullivan instructed jurors they could not take Jim's reputation into consideration.

Deere had two witnesses: Arthur Howerton, a Fort Worth police detective, and Baxter Honey of Lubbock. Both testified that Thomas was a dangerous killer. Honey recounted his wounds Thomas inflicted during their gunfight. Howerton said he knew many of Thomas's associates, two of whom were "shot in the back of the head twice. If Jim didn't like a person, he would get rid of him by killing him.

The courthouse custodian, Walton, testified that he had heard two shots from Deere's house shortly after he had arrived at his home. Deere testified in his own defense.

"I shot Jim Thomas because I was afraid he would kill me," he told jurors.

During their closing arguments, prosecutors painted Deere as a killer hired by Fort Worth criminals.

His case went to the jury on November 12. After three hours of deliberation, jurors were evenly split. Deere remained free on bond.

Mills, the district attorney, remained convinced Deere had not told the whole story. Regarding public opinion on the trial's outcome, Mills said, "I do not know whether a new trial would be set. We may not try him again." Mills was always convinced it was more than an argument and said that Jim's palm hat was on top of Deere's piano, indicating Thomas had been invited in.

Deere remained in legal limbo for eight years, waiting for the D.A.'s office to set a new trial date, which it never did. In January 1959, he went before Judge Sam Sullivan without an attorney to request dismissal of the murder charge. Sullivan dismissed the charge.

Deere died in October 1979 and is buried in Durant. The house where Thomas died is gone, with only aged oak trees where it once stood. A piece of the original sidewalk still runs in front of the empty lot.

No Justice

Six years earlier, on January 8, 1953, the Nolan County district attorney asked the court to dismiss the criminal case against Thomas because he was dead. The court granted the request.

The panel truck Jim Thomas bought from Hubert Deere.

The Portal to Texas History, University of North Texas Libraries Special Collections

Jim Thomas after being questioned by police
about the death of Lon Holley in March 1948.

University of Texas at Arlington Libraries, Special Collections

Jim Thomas' house in Fort Worth.
Christena Stephens

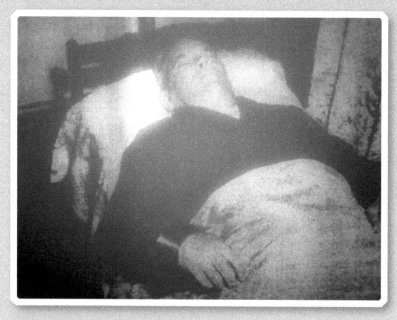

Jim Thomas in the funeral home before his body was transported to Dallas.
Christena Stephens

··· **PART FIVE** ···

WHAT WENT WRONG

CRIMINALS AND SCIENCE

During one of my early presentations on the Hunt murders, a lady in the audience asked me about forensics and whether the bodies could be exhumed to acquire DNA. The question surprised me and led me to research the scientific tools available to these investigators to help solve this case.

The investigations into the Hunt murders and the earlier attack on Roy Hunt were led by a small-town sheriff and a few Texas Rangers that had never encountered cases of these magnitudes. Quite simply, they did not use the forensic technology available at the time to its full advantage. While comparing their investigative skills to an unflawed investigation would be imprudent, understanding how far along forensic science had advanced by the 1940s gives further depth at how many questions remain unanswered in both cases.

By 1932, labs could analyze blood, identify firearms, decipher gunpowder patterns, examine bombs and explosives, identify tool marks, examine documents, perform cryptanalysis (cryptographic writings), and conduct chemical and toxicological examinations. Even handwriting and document analyses were emerging tools in this new science.

Texas Governor James Allred's main platform in the mid-1930s was improving and making law enforcement more accountable. Under his governorship, the Texas Department of Safety (TDS) was established in 1935, which included the creation of a scientific crime laboratory. The Texas Rangers and the Highway Patrol were also placed under TDS. Allred's Governorship helped develop forensics as a crime-solving tool.

However, even with all the forensic science testing capabilities for solving crimes, both then and now, not all science was or is accurate in any field, particularly forensics. However, many criminal cases would have and would remain unsolved if it was not for forensics.

Take, for instance, a bullet affects a body in many ways, but this effect comes down to the caliber, speed, flight direction, and the part of the body the bullet hits. Without forensic ballistic science, the only investigative aspect that could be determined was that the person had been shot. Ballistics as a science first emerged in 1926. By the 1930s, this field had advanced significantly. Scientists could determine caliber, manufacturer, and the possible gun or rifle from which the bullet was fired.

Ballistic science also provides insight into whether the bullet is high velocity, creating a clean hole without fractures, or low velocity, causing fractures and deforming the area where the bullet entered. In addition, by examining a bullet, ballistics experts can match it to a weapon by deciphering the gun barrel's interior, cuts, or imprints—a series of spiral grooves on the bullet as it is spinning out of the barrel.

By the 1930s, fingerprints had become the gold standard in solving crimes. Science had determined the unique friction ridge patterns on our fingertips, which are defined by the fine lines forming arches, loops, and whorls. Everything touched by bare human hands leaves fingerprint evidence behind. In the 1940s, fingerprints were the only sure-fire forensic evidence because they could prove an offender was at a crime scene. This science had already been used for nearly sixty years by the time of the Hunt crimes.

The first use of fingerprints in the United States was in 1882, when Gilbert Thompson with the U.S. Geological Survey used them to prevent forgeries of commissary orders during a survey in New Mexico. Fingerprints became used in 1903 to identify criminals at the Sing Sing Prison in New York.

By 1904, the U.S. Department of Justice established a fingerprint bureau in Leavenworth, Kansas. It began with the fingerprints of federal prisoners and expanded as an exchange service so records could be circulated among law enforcement. Eventually, this led to the creation of the FBI's National Division of Identification and Information. By mid-1929, this system had more than 1.7 million records.

Footprint and tire track impressions also became a constant investigative tool during the 1940s. Investigators had developed a set of analytical characteristics to help identify brands of shoes or tires, although these identifications could be subjective due to the examiner's experience and education.

Impression evidence was and still is supposed to identify the source of the impression by ascertaining a set of characteristics. By the 1940s, impression evidence of casts or drawings constituted most forensic examinations at crime scenes. Unfortunately, consistency was the hardest to control in both the casts and the drawings.

Footprints offered useful information, depending on the surface where the print was made and the person's progression. For example, tracks on sand are smaller than the actual foot; tracks in mud are larger. Footprints made by a person running are smaller than if the same person is walking. Moreover, tracks also can reveal physical defects, such as a limp.

Tire tracks were harder to determine because retreading tires was popular during the 1930s and 1940s, although many crimes at the time were solved based solely on tire marks.

Tires are manufactured with physical features, such as blocks and grooves that can leave impressions either in relief (positive) or as an impression (negative), with the latter being the most outstanding feature. Back wheels in the 1930s and 1940s left heavier tracks. Other tire identifiers include scars made from driving over a sharp stone, a piece of iron, or glass. Those scars could be easily determined in tire tracks.

Peripheral evidence—like nylon, polyester, acrylic, wool, and cotton fibers discovered at crime scenes—were harder to identify at the time of the Hunt murders because they could only be examined either by the naked eye or under a microscope. Back then, techniques for identifying fibers were limited. Investigators could only determine the type of fiber, and perhaps patterns, such as designs or tear marks, that might link one fiber to another. Investigators could also study the quality, diameter, and color to determine if they came from the same source.

Witness testimony was also handled differently in the 1940s. Often, prosecutors did not interview them before a trial. The lead investigator secured witnesses, and their testimonies were reduced to a small, signed summary and turned over to the prosecutor.

While many greeted forensics with reverence, the science is susceptible to human error. Forensic science was still young in the 1930s and 1940s, and evidence often boiled down to observed facts and using what was considered exceptional judgment to draw conclusions about potential evidence. Irrelevant facts should have had no part in any case; however, they often made it into the courtroom. Innocent people went to prison or even the electric chair based on investigative errors.

Evidence always bears the personality and professional mark of the person who gathered it. Processing crime scenes varied widely across Texas based on investigative techniques, jurisdictions, inconsistent policies, and bias. Honest mistakes were made due to haste, inexperience, or a lack of investigative skills. In the end, an investigator's duty at a crime scene is to the victim. Yes, despite the serious forensic deficiencies of the time, and the lack of experience of the investigating officers, any forensic evidence was better than a gut feeling in solving a crime, particularly a double murder.

25

LEADS NOT
FOLLOWED

Investigators in the Hunt cases focused on two pieces of physical evidence in the Hunt murders: the buffed tennis shoes found in the Veazey house and two pieces of string from the Hunt home likely left behind by the murderer. But investigators also discounted evidence that could have led to another possible killer.

The investigations of both Thomas and the Newtons were rife with inadequacies, mainly due to investigators' lack of follow-up.

In both the shooting and the murders, investigators, including the Texas Rangers, D.A. LaFont, and Sherriff Hutson had credible leads that they did not explore. Even a private investigation firm hired by the Hunt family received vital information that was ignored. The Rangers' files on the case hold scant information about the crimes.

Discounted Discoveries

By August 1944, all the Hunt cases had been transferred to Hale County. Remarkably, both Billy Newton and Jim Thomas appeared together in a jam-packed Plainview courtroom on August 7, when Judge Russell set their respective trial dates. Two Texas Rangers, Raymond Waters and Norvell Redwine, flanked Thomas, while Billy was surrounded by his four attorneys. According to newspaper accounts, the men acted like complete strangers, and the Rangers never noted their reactions to each other.

However, a connection between Roy and Billy came to light in early 1943, when Raymond Tallant, a Dallas real estate agent, became involved with both doctors on behalf of Matilda Newton. A friend of Billy's father, Tallant was acting as a mediator between the men to help avoid a trial. Matilda asked him to investigate the rumored affair between Roy and Ruth.

Tallant told the Texas Rangers that his only interest in the case was as a Good Samaritan trying to patch up differences between the men. Apparently, both doctors conveyed to Tallant that they were not mad at each other. Billy said he had not seen Hunt in nine years and insisted he did not shoot Roy.

Tallant told Billy that Roy would drop all charges if Billy paid Roy $10,000 for time lost from his practice because of the shooting. Tallant then asked Roy why he had been shot. Roy was circumspect, and nothing came from Tallant's effort to shed light on Billy's case, a motive for the shooting, or whether the affair happened.

Investigation Misses

Uninvestigated leads in both cases primarily dealt with Billy. The doctor owned a Stinson Model 105 Voyager plane, but investigators never checked gas receipts or the airport flight logs to determine if he used his plane to fly from the Temple airport on May 20, 1942.

D.A. LaFont and Ranger Gault decided which leads, out of the dozens they received, were worth pursuing. But in some cases, they failed to cover basic investigative procedures. They never searched Billy's home in Cameron, for example.

Gault remained convinced Billy framed his alibi well in advance. Then he dropped his alibi because Roy survived the shooting and positively identified him. Gault even commented to LaFont that it would be a good idea to do a little investigation in Cameron to determine Billy's defense. However, none of the files show any effort was made to do so.

On July 23, 1942, nearly two months after the attempted shooting, Gault received a hand-written informant note from the Milam County Sheriff, Sara White. It stated that Billy's car had a hole in the right rear door, near the door handle. Emory Camp, the Newtons' lawyer, allegedly fixed the door in May at a place in Cameron. This, too, was never investigated or presented during the trials. Nor did investigators interview close friends or acquaintances of Billy and Roy.

At one-point Gault remarked to LaFont that the phone calls from Lubbock to Littlefield and Cameron to Littlefield needed investigation, but this was not done until March 1944, almost two years after Roy's shooting. That March, Texas Ranger Joe Thompson discovered from a confidential source at Southwestern Bell in Temple that no records existed of Billy placing long-distance calls to or from Cameron anytime between May 19 and May 21.

Texas Ranger Tom Brown, Jr. also searched Southwestern Bell's phone records in 1944 and verified four calls Roy received at his home on May 20. Brown found no calls placed on May 21. The first call to Roy on that night was at 7:55 p.m. and originated from a pay telephone at the Santa Fe Depot in Lubbock.

On a second try at 7:56 p.m., the caller was told that Roy was expected in about thirty minutes. The caller asked the operator to hold the ticket for later. The caller's name was not recorded. No one answered at 8:34 p.m. However, at 8:36 p.m., a call lasted three minutes and fifty-one seconds. A subsequent call was placed from the same number at 10:47 p.m. and lasted three minutes and one second. Because of the long delay in investigating the calls, the operator could not remember if the caller was a man or woman.

Another lead that was never pursued involved John Rainey of Cameron, who was driving a grain truck to Lubbock on the night of the shooting. At 9 a.m. on May 19, 1942, he and Martin Susik left Cameron for Lubbock Economy Mills to unload thrashed kaffir. Rainey said they passed a car between Trent and Abilene. Both men told investigators Billy was driving when the car passed them going west between 2:30 p.m. and 3:00 p.m. Both men said the car had two occupants.

Anonymous handwritten or typed letters from Cameron were sent to Roy's brother, Ewell, and LaFont after the first shooting. One was written on the back of an envelope. Most of the handwriting was shaky and uneven, but they indicated Billy was known for his temper. One, which arrived six days after the shooting, claimed that Billy "has threatened nearly every man with whom he has had any intimate contact," and in an apparent reference to Roy, that Billy "repeatedly told people he would kill the dirty son of a bitch and throw his body in the river. His father killed a man in this county, and this could never be proven." Once again, these allegations were never investigated.

Private Investigators

Early in the investigation of the murders, the Hunt family grew frustrated with the lack of progress. Investigators and LaFont offered little more than the occasional tidbit of information to placate the Hunts. In late 1945, the family hired Smith and Wenig, a private investigation firm in Dallas. They outlined specific questions that investigators wouldn't answer, especially whether Billy was involved in the murders.

The firm purportedly traveled all over Texas to determine motives in both cases, uncover links between Billy and Thomas, and discover who was paying Thomas's attorneys. The firm came up with no substantial leads and discovered nothing that provided evidence or new information related to the shooting or the murders.

The firm's final report indicated specific interviews should be conducted, but neither the firm nor law officers ever did them. In addition, the report suggested witnesses in Amarillo, such as Red Craig, had not told investigators everything they knew, but this finding was also ignored.

The firm even received a tip that it should interview Ruth at her parents' Clarendon home about a possible motive in the Hunt murders, but once again the firm never followed through. The reports also suggested the Dean of the Galveston Medical School, who knew both doctors, should be interviewed, but he never was.

Each witness the private investigators interviewed provided additional information, which became a report filler. Overall, what was mostly gathered were routine character references for Thomas, the Newtons, and Roy. Some of the interviewees said they feared for their safety, and others seemed scared, investigators noted.

The most remarkable bit of information they discovered was that after she was arraigned in the shooting, Ruth visited Roy at the Littlefield hospital, and when she entered his room, he took hold of her hand and remarked he had no idea why her husband would attempt to kill him.

The private investigators completed their report in February 1946 and billed the Hunt family $1,581.05 for thirty days of work, including sixteen travel days. Everything the firm gathered came down to rumors, hearsay, or facts that were already known. They established no definitive proof to explain why Billy would have shot Roy. Nor could they say who had murdered the Hunts or why.

The Santa Fe Depot in Lubbock, where the call to Roy Hunt
originated the night he was shot by Billy Newton.
Lubbock County Historical Commission

FORENSICS AND CONJECTURES

After the question about DNA evidence, I concentrated on the forensics—or the lack of it. Little concrete evidence was turned over to the Austin lab or presented in court for either of the Hunt cases.

In the Newton trials, the state presented not one piece of physical or forensic evidence. His convictions were based solely on Hunt's testimony that he gave while he was still alive.

In the murder case, the state presented forty-six pieces of evidence, focused on the tire tracks, footprints, and fiber evidence, even though the killer used a gun, string, and possibly chloroform. The appeals court ruled the state's evidence was not enough to uphold Thomas's convictions.

During Thomas's trials, Norvell Redwine and Aubrey Fawver identified the state exhibits entered into evidence. Redwine testified the evidence removed from the bodies was placed in his hands, and he gave them to Joe Fletcher, Chief of the Bureau of Records and Identification for the Department of Public Safety in Austin.

The state entered into evidence Thomas's clothing, the tennis shoes, bits of cord and paper, the wire used to tie the Hunts' arms and legs together, the belt taken from their ankles, fishing cord that had been tied around their wrists, an electric wire that had been tied around Mae's legs, two plaster casts of footprints found near the Hunt residence, coat hangers, pieces of the gate from the backyard, and part of a car fender. None of it tied Thomas to the murders.

The state made a circumstantial case against Thomas that relied on expert witnesses. Prosecutors argued the car tracks found near the scene of the Hunt murders were similar to those of a car to which Thomas had access, that he wore tennis shoes from an Amarillo residence, and that the two pieces of string, which almost fit together, connected him to the Hunt homicides.

Tire Tracks

One foremost piece of evidence was a tire track left near the laundry, about three hundred feet from the Hunt home. If you were standing at the laundry, you could easily see the front of the Hunt house. The Texas Rangers and local officers speculated a car pulled into the alley, allowing the driver to view the Hunt home. Based on this speculation, is how Levi Duncan connected the car to the murders with a single car track.

He traced footprints coming out of the laundry's back door to a tire track in the alley south of the laundry, concluding the car drove from the north to the side street on the east. Duncan's testimony stated he could see where the left wheel cut under and backed up in the alley, backed east, and then went up the alley about twenty feet. The left front and right rear tracks were the clearest, with only the left tire tracks being complete.

Duncan measured the track impression as 5-1/4 inches across. The outside ribs, which are the part of the tire tread pattern created by grooves running around the tire, were wider, at about 1-1/16 inches. The next two ribs on the outside and inside were 3/4 inches wide, and a middle rib, which is the narrowest, was 5/8 of an inch. On the outside of each of the 1-1/16 tracks was a square-shaped dent that measured 7/16 inches deep and 1-1/2 inches across.

In addition, he noticed a crease between each rib was a quarter of an inch in diameter across. The four creases each extended out a tit (a tire whisker) and were 1-7/8 inches apart. Furthermore, the creases each had two tits that faced outward from the tire.

According to Duncan's observations, this indicated the right rear wheel of the car had hit and run up on the piece of concrete in the alley, leaving behind black marks on the rock. This concrete piece was fourteen inches wide and twelve inches high.

Without telling anyone what he was doing, Duncan diagrammed the track and took it to a Lubbock tire shop. Comparing it with tires for sale at the store, he concluded it was a Lee tire based on the width of five-and-a-quarter inches. He then confirmed his finding from the shop's tire book. A few days later, Duncan saw the Craig car in Amarillo on 6th Street and noticed it had a Lee tire on the right front wheel. He also noticed both the running board and the fender were bent and scratched, allowing him to put the damage and the rock together. No photographs were taken of the tire tracks or the tires.

In his testimonies, Duncan said the tire tracks corresponded to the right front tire of the Craig car based on the measurements and tread of tire tracks in the alley. He indicated that both the size of the track and the Lee tire were the same size.

Duncan testified that Craig's car had the same style of Lee tire on the left front, and that it matched the tracks in the alley. "I don't say that that tire is the tire that made the tracks down there. I say that that made a similar track," he stated.

He further stated in the trials that he understood the tires on the car had been switched after Craig's wife had a blowout. He never recalled whether the tires were switched before or after the murders.

Footprints

Numerous footprints were found outside the Hunt home. Investigators concluded the footprints found outside the Hunt home were made by the same person, who was wearing tennis shoes and not boots as previously indicated at the beginning of the investigation.

"I saw tracks around the Hunt home, and right behind the home, it was a loose, sandy soil right around the windows of the nursery. I couldn't tell which way they were going. I also saw tracks around the window, close to Dr. Hunt's bedroom," Sheriff Hutson testified.

In the crime scene photo of the nursery, dead grass was under those windows, not loose dirt.

Aubrey Fawver testified he traced the tracks from the east side of the house, near the Hunts' bedroom window, through the alley behind the home to the westside street, and back through a garden to the northwest corner of the garage. He said the track imprint on the seat of the child's chair outside the nursery window was similar to all those tracks.

Despite the abundance of tracks, only two preservation casts were made—one right footprint found about twenty feet north of the alley, at the rear of the home in a sandy, soft soil with no grass; and a left footprint found about four feet from the first one. No photographs were taken of the foot tracks.

During the trials, the state established that Thomas had been a guest at the Sid Veazey home in Amarillo on the days leading up to the murders and probably had access to Alvis Veazey's tennis shoes. The shoes were taken as evidence from the home, and prosecutors alleged that Jim placed them back in Alvis' closet after the murders.

At the Nolan County trial, Alvis identified the shoes as his size nine basketball shoes. While he did not say they had been buffed, he indicated they had been scratched close to the bottom of the arch of the shoe, with the side of the left shoe appearing to have been buffed. He noted the shoes exhibited natural wear and tear on the bottom of the heel and toe area caused by stopping and starting.

Sid testified his garage repaired tubes and not tires. He did have a buffing machine with a six-inch emery wheel on one side and a six-inch buffer on the other side. He testified that neither machine would leave the marks found on those shoes.

The state built its case around Thomas going into the garage and using the tire buffing machine to alter the soles early in the morning of October 26 so they would not match the casts the officers made outside the Hunt home.

In expert testimony on both the tracks and the tennis shoes, George Gambill, with the Identification Bureau of the Texas Department of Public Safety, testified that the designs of Alvis' shoes were similar to the plaster casts of footprints taken near the Hunt home. But they were not a match because the shoes had been buffed.

Referencing this comparison is Gambill's Nolan County testimony:

> I made an examination of these casts and shoes. The cast I found by measurement and by observation were made by a shoe with the same design these shoes have. The design in both the heel in the sole is the same design. The V-shaped markings are in the same location as the ones on the shoe and all of these markings here are in the same location. They have the same angles and in fact where it can be measured they measure within one-hundredth of an inch on the cast and on the shoe. As closely as they can be measured they are exactly the same size and shape. I did not measure the cast as to length and make a comparison with the shoes. I don't believe I measured from the heel of the cast to the toe of the cast either. I did not examine the shoe as to its size.
>
> There is a discrepancy which existed on both casts and there are not raised places in the cast which are not present on the shoe because there is three noticeable bars in the cast. In my opinion, some type of abrasive has been used on this shoe. This shoe appears to me to have been buffed in this area right here. It doesn't show normal wear as it does in the sole.
>
> By bars, I mean where the bar appears to have been when the track was made and are not present on the shoes at this time on the instep. This is the place where it appears to have been buffed. If those shoes on the night of October 25 or the morning of October 26 were in the same condition as I now find them, they couldn't have made the tracks represented by the casts that have been introduced in evidence. Any Hood shoe would have the same design upon them.

Upon cross-examination, he testified:

> Now, on this right shoe it doesn't have the same appearance as it
> has here in back in this portion. It's clean and looks like it was freshly
> knocked off from the rubber. This I refer to is on the right shoe just
> about the instep on the outside and on the right-hand side of the
> shoe. It seems to have been made by some buffing machine or some
> grinding or sandpaper or something of that kind.

Under redirect examination, Gambill further testified:

> It's my opinion these shoes as they are now could not have made
> the tracks shown on these casts because there are bars as I call them
> present on the cast that is not present on the shoe and these bars are
> in the same place appear to have been buffed.

During the trials and appeals, Thomas's lawyers emphasized that
the state never proved their client wore the shoes, only that he had an
opportunity to wear them. Only at the Nolan County trial, when his
shoe size came into testimony, did the state attempt to prove Thomas
could have worn the shoes. Then Gault testified Jim wore an eight-
and-a-half-size shoe. The defense called lawyer Temple Dickson,who
verified the shoes Thomas was wearing during the trial were indeed a
size nine and a half.

String

The state's strongest evidence linking Thomas to the murders was a
piece of string found toward the foot of the Hunts' bed. It was partly
resting on the bed rail and on the comforter covering the bodies.

Five days after the murders, officers searching the Veazey garage
found another piece of string on a stove in Amarillo. Potter County
Deputy Sheriff Vaughn found the tiny piece of string during a second
search of the garage. It was laying an oil barrel gas stove grate about
six or eight inches from the bottom. He took the string to the sheriff's
office and placed it in an envelope, which was later taken to Austin.

Prosecutors inferred the string had been cut from one of several
bonds tying the Hunts' bodies together. They argued Thomas found

the two-inch string in his pocket after he had returned to the Veazey residence and pitched it onto the stove to destroy it.

Three witnesses gave expert testimonies on these strings. Fawver sent the string found on the Hunts' bed to the Austin laboratory. On cross-examination during the trials, he said he had not inspected it under a microscope and could not say whether it was any different from the "great balls of such cord in stores or whether it had independent characteristics."

Gambill, a state identifications expert, said the strings matched in fiber grade, thread count, diameter, and the depth of a cut where a sharp instrument had sliced partly through it before being torn jaggedly the rest of the way. He concluded this after examining various lengths and diameters of strings with magnifying glasses, microscopes, and graduated rulers. Glen McLaughlin, a chemist for the Texas Department of Public Safety, testified for the state at the Dawson trial that the strings and the cuts on them were similar. While he could not say they were from the same cord, they could have been because of the similar nature of the cuts.

In the Dawson County case, he stated that the two string pieces were delivered to him on October 29, 1943, and November 1, 1943. After examining them with a naked eye and a microscope, he concluded the pieces were of similar fiber, along with having the same degree of twist and firmness. The cuts were similar under both examination methods. The most important part of his testimony was demonstrating that the strings could not be placed back together where they would match one another. During cross-examination, McLaughlin testified he could not state that both strings were from the same piece of cord.

His Nolan County trial testimony slightly differed on the methods of examination. He received and examined both strings on November 1, 1943, with two types of microscopes, along with micrometer calipers, which measured the thickness of the two pieces of string. He stated both pieces were composed of cotton fibers and had the same number of woven strands. Then he demonstrated to the jurors that the strings as they were would not fit back together.

The evidence presented in Thomas's trials was weak and circumstantial. It only inadvertently connected him to the murders. Prosecutors did not produce for jurors the fatal bullet that ended Roy's life.

Expert witnesses in the lower courts gave their scientific opinions at the time based on their evolving special knowledge—knowledge that impressed these juries enough to convict Thomas. Yet, none of this evidence was conclusive enough for the appeals court to uphold Thomas's convictions.

SILENT WITNESS

The photographs in the Hunt murder case are only a meager glimpse of the horrific crime. They are a silent witness. The photos should have told the story with little need for interpretation.

Law enforcement began using photography at crime scenes as early as 1859. By the late nineteenth century, photos were used to take mug shots.

Gradually, photographs became an essential aid in investigations, especially in homicide cases. In many cases, photographs preserved the conditions at a crime scene exactly as the criminal had left it. Even today, photos provide an overview of the crime and record any evidence upon which future testimony may be based. They carry evidentiary weight to help attorneys present their cases to jurors.

In detective movies from the 1940s, crime scenes are often punctuated by the flashing of camera blubs. This was not the case at the Hunt home after the murders. The photographers lacked training in photographing murder cases, and they received little to no instruction from the investigators.

Basics—photographing the scene from all possible angles, capturing everything that could be used as evidence and getting close-ups of the bodies to show their injuries—were overlooked.

At that time, photos should have had reference points for the contents of each picture. The case name, date, hour, light conditions, film, lens, camera used, length of exposure, and aperture used should have been written on the back of the images. The Hunt photos had none.

While it was common for local law enforcement to engage an outside photographer, as they did in this case, the practice often delayed the investigation and could disturb the crime scene. Smaller departments in the 1940s could not afford to have a paid photographer or an officer trained to take photos. In the Hunt investigation, Sherriff Hutson called Aubrey Fawver, who then called Lubbock reporter Ed Watson to take the initial photographs. Fawver later took some images himself, but it was never clear who shot which photographs at the Hunt home.

Photos must have a clear relevance in a case, with the trial judge determining their overall pertinence. Photograph relevancy boils down to whether an image can assist the jury in understanding the case or help witnesses explain their testimony. The jury ultimately decides a photograph's value and relevance. A jury often can decipher information from a good photograph as if they were physically at the crime scene itself.

Jim Thomas's attorneys tried to prevent the state from introducing any photographs. Even with so few presented, the defense fretted the photos would distress the jurors and prejudice them against Thomas.

Hunt Crime Scene Photos

In 1943, the Hunt case photographs became an incomplete archive of the gruesome murders, and investigators did not employ these silent witnesses to their maximum potential.

Only ten crime scene photos were taken during the entire Hunt investigation.

Three images show the Hunts' bodies from the angles of an east view of the bed, a view from the north of their bound legs, and another north view of Roy's profile.

One photograph was taken of the casting process of a single foot-print near the Hunt home and only one photo was shot of the south nursery window, where the killer entered the home.

A single photograph was taken of the nursery closet, and a long-range, unfocused photo was taken of the nearby laundry where investigators at one time alleged the killer had waited for the Hunts to retire for the night. One photo showed the southern view of the alley behind the Hunt home, but no reason was given for taking it.

A portion of the concrete that the killer's car supposedly backed into was also photographed with the Texas Ranger pointing at it, but the wide-angle image was out of focus.

Only one image of the Craig car that Jim Thomas allegedly borrowed showed a distant view of the scratch and dent on the fender allegedly caused by the piece of concrete. The photographer did not capture a closeup of the damage, and the photo was out of focus, weakly framed, and overexposed along the edges.

No wide-angle or close-up shots of the tire tracks or footprints were taken, nor were there any images of the Lee tire. Although it was alleged the killer broke down the back gate when leaving the Hunt premises, no photos were taken to document this evidence. There also were no wide-angle photos of the Hunts' bedroom or the closet.

No close-up shot was taken of the little red metal chair showing the dent and the killer's footprint. In addition, there were no photos of the items used to bind the Hunts, no close-up of their wounds, especially of Mae's face, no south view image of their heads, and no shots of the home's interior to document the layout of the house.

None of the photos included a simple ruler to provide a size reference in any of the photos. Most interestingly, no photographs were taken or introduced into evidence of the Veazey garage, the buffing wheel, or the tennis shoes. And most damning to the investigation, no photograph was taken of the bullet that killed Roy.

However, what the existing photographs do reveal is significant. The east view of the bodies shows Mae's hands had a slight contraction because of the brain injury from her head trauma. It also reveals a deep bruise on Mae's left forearm, indicating she was held down with enough force to cause the bruise before she died. Unfortunately, the photographer's camera malfunctioned because the image appears double exposed.

A chilling photo of the nursery window shows that the screen was meticulously removed and leaned against the back wall of the house. The screen had two hooks at the top and a latch at the bottom. To remove it, the killer had to have had all his materials in a bag or in his pockets, including the gun.

Then the nursery window was opened to its highest point. The cord for the window blind was pulled through the open window, with the blinds raised halfway. No dirt was found around the window, and the backyard was covered with dead grass, which does not corroborate Sheriff Hutson's testimony about loose, sandy soil around the nursery window. Some investigators led everyone to believe the killer stood outside the Hunts' east bedroom window waiting for them to turn off the lights, but no photo was taken of that window.

The state admitted two crime scene photos during the Dawson County trial: one of the east view of the Hunts' bodies and another of the south nursery window. According to Fawver's testimony, Watson took all the photos at the house under his supervision. Fawver then took possession of the film and transported it to the Lubbock Police Department, where he developed it.

Fawver further testified the photographs reflected the scene as it existed when the pictures were taken. He continued to testify that nothing had been disturbed. He said the pictures reflected the condition of the bedspread and the location of the chair outside the nursery window. However, Hutson told reporters that as soon as he walked into the bedroom, he picked up the bedspread and covered the bodies.

In the Nolan County trial, five photos were introduced, and Fawver's testimony dramatically changed. He said he—not Watson— took the photos introduced as evidence. According to his testimony, nothing had been disturbed in the bedroom, other than the silk comforter, which had been pulled back from the Hunts' feet. Levi Duncan noted on the witness stand that Fawver took the photo of the concrete, which the killer allegedly backed into, on November 6, 1943, nine days after investigators identified it as possible evidence. Fawver also said he took the Craig automobile photo the same day.

Jim Thomas's defense attorneys objected to photos of the bodies submitted in all three trials, especially over the east view image of the bodies, because they were "a gruesome and ghastly spectacle of the disfigured, maimed, manacled, and mangled dead bodies of the Hunts."

The defense also argued the pictures did not prove any disputed issues in the case and did nothing to illustrate the state's case or inform the jury. Their only purpose, the attorneys said, was to prejudice jurors against Thomas.

The court overruled all the defense objections at the trials, saying the pictures speak for themselves and allowed the jury to see the photos.

In this murder case, the photography mistakes were negligent oversights on many levels. First, why was a reporter from the *Lubbock Avalanche-Journal* employed to take the important crime scene photos, instead of calling the Littlefield newspaper photographer? Second, only three photos were taken of the bedroom crime scene, which had been disturbed by Hutson and tramped on by over thirty onlookers. More photographs should have been taken, not just of the murder scene, but of the entire house to document the condition of the residence when officers first arrived.

Finally, the photographer should have been told to shoot each piece of evidence—the tire tracks, footprints, and each item used to tie up the Hunts, along with a close-up photo of Mae and one of the bullet that killed Roy. Most importantly, a photo of the Hunts' bedroom closet should have also been taken, along with an inside photo of the nursery window.

Without these images, it is impossible to analyze what evidence may have been overlooked. In the end, these ten photographs failed at supporting any circumstantial evidence against Jim Thomas.

PART SIX

SUMMATION

QUESTIONS, QUESTIONS, QUESTIONS

Murder was no stranger to the quintessential town of Littlefield. In 1937, Leroy Kelley killed Sheriff Loyd in a drunken delirium. Not much evidence was needed to prove Kelley was a killer because he admitted on the witness stand that if he shot Loyd, then he needed punishing. The most important fact from Kelley's case was that the doctor who removed the fatal bullet from Loyd's spinal column brought it to court, and the state introduced it into evidence while he was on the witness stand.

Sherriff Hutson and Judge Russell were both key figures in Kelley's case. Both men later played significant roles in the shooting of Roy Hunt and the later murder of him and his wife.

By the 1940s, forensics became more readily available for police to use. The Texas Rangers were progressive enough for them to work cohesively to investigate crimes, especially murder case investigations. All these law enforcement men were expected to be professional in their work ethics. Most importantly, these Rangers had the opportunity to utilize available science to solve a crime by collecting evidence at a crime scene.

Investigators are supposed to find evidence so convincing that no reasonable doubt exists for a jury.

Forensics have evolved over the decades, based on lab-tested methods, and these methods are explained by expert testimony based on unbiased scientific findings.

Investigators have a responsibility to avoid convicting—let alone getting a death sentence—for the wrong person. English jurist William Blackstone's ratio— "[B]etter that ten guilty persons escape than that one innocent suffer"—was needed more than ever in this case.

Investigative Failures

Investigative failures led to more questions than answers in both Hunt cases. Who killed the Hunts? Why were they killed? Did Billy Newton attempt to kill Roy?

Beginning with Roy's attempted murder in May 1942, the Newtons' alibis were supported by witnesses who swore they saw the couple hundreds of miles away from Littlefield on that night. But law enforcement did not collect evidence at the scene, in the hospital, or in the city of Cameron. Why did they not search for tire tracks or footprints? Why did they not test the doctor's guns for a recent firing or bullet comparison? What happened to the two bullets taken out of Roy's body? Why were those bullets not introduced as evidence in Billy's trials, as the bullet was in Kelley's case?

Relying only on Roy's testimony and his hospital statements that Billy shot him while he talked to Ruth Newton, without any corroborating evidence, weakened the prosecutors' case significantly. Roy Hunt's testimony also raises key questions, such as why he could not recall the make of the car he was leaning on while talking to Ruth.

Why, after nine years since last seeing Roy, would the Newtons drive over four hundred miles to Littlefield to kill him? What was their motive? Sherriff Hutson and D.A. LaFont had initially suggested Billy may have found out his oldest child was not his. Most importantly, why did Roy never explain why he went to see Ruth, even when asked in court? What made him leave the house late at night, get in his car, and drive east of Littlefield? Why did he never reveal Ruth's reason for calling?

If the killer intended to shoot Roy, why did he not follow Roy out into the field with the flashlight taken from the car? Why would the shooter not pursue the unarmed, wounded Roy to determine if he was dead?

While Roy's testimony is solid, the case against Billy would have been stronger if other physical evidence had been presented during his trials. In the end, twenty-four jurors found him guilty based on Roy's testimony alone. Why did Ruth maintain her silence, even after she left her husband?

The murders raise even more questions. Investigators never found a murder weapon—or weapons. Based on powder burns, Roy was shot in the head at point-blank range, resulting in instant death. If Mae awoke at the same time as her husband, why did the assailant not shoot her, too, so that he could get away from the house as quickly as possible? Was it because the killer did not intend to murder her? Her response to Jo Ann indicated something else was going on inside the bedroom. Why else were her panties laid across her and Roy's necks? In those days, rape was a taboo topic, even if it could be proven.

Tying up the couple so meticulously and in such a grotesque manner ensured that if they were not dead, they could not have escaped their bonds. The binding took a long time—not a few minutes, as speculated by the investigators. Stripping the insulation off a light cord, finding neckties, cutting string and fishing cord, and unwinding wire hangers to bind the couple was laborious and time consuming. In addition, the killer could not have tied up the bodies so intricately in the dark. What was the underlying purpose for all the various forms of binding? Could the killer have wanted to demonstrate power over the couple? Could it have been a peculiar endeavor that only meant something to the killer?

Then there's an even bigger question—what if murder was never the intention? What if the killer intended to tie up Roy and make him watch, helplessly, while his wife was raped? Was the binding done to give the assailant time to get away from the house under the cover of darkness?

The mishandling of the investigation began as soon as investigators arrived. The fundamental rule is to not disturb the crime scene until all investigators have arrived and photographs have been taken.

Sheriff Hutson ignored this rule as soon as he stepped into the bedroom and threw the bedspread over the couple. He then turned around and used their phone to call other investigators. So had Lou Grissom.

While the Hunts' body positions were described in detail, the descriptions have no reference to other objects in the room. The victims' wounds, even trivial ones, should have been fully noted, but the scratches on Mae's arm were not recorded and were only later noted by the funeral director. The deep bruise on her right arm was never described, even though it proved she had been forcibly held down before she died.

One of the most significant investigative mistakes was having doctors related to the victims perform the post-mortem examinations. To provide unbiased information on the state of the bodies, the examinations should have been conducted by a neutral party, not by Roy's brother, Ewell, and his friend and co-worker, Dr. Janes. The emotional turmoil these men endured while conducting their examinations must have been incomprehensible and certainly haunted them for the rest of their lives.

Another critical oversight was that investigators never searched Roy's office at the hospital. His office remained locked and dark.

In the 1940s, the platinum standard for placing anyone at a crime scene was fingerprints. Except for Roy's, no other fingerprints were reported at the Hunt home, not even Mae's or other family or guests. That immediately throws up a red flag because there were guests in the house the night before the murders. If any comparison fingerprint testing of those guests or others who had contact with the crime scene was done, no records or mentions of the tests exist. If Jim Thomas was the murderer, why were his fingerprints not found at the house? They were already on file at the FBI and were used to identify him in the Hastings Bank Robbery. While the killer could have worn gloves, it would have been difficult to bind the bodies so intricately—especially using string—with covered hands.

What about all the other evidence collected at the crime scene? Out of the forty-six pieces of evidence gathered in the Hunt investigation, only seventeen were introduced during Thomas's trials. Significant evidence not presented included the bullet, Mae's nightgown and panties, Roy's neckties and handkerchief, the fishing cord, bed linens, dirt samples, pieces of wood from the back gate, and a buffer wheel and grinders from the Veazey garage.

Mae's and Jo Ann's bed clothing was sent to Austin, but no lab report was presented on their clothing or other evidentiary trace evidence, such as hair, bodily fluids, or chloroform. Investigators never noted the arrangement of the clothes, their color or material type, or whether they were soaked, dry, or torn. Roy's pajamas were never recorded or collected into evidence. Even the appeals court noted the omission and asked why the bedclothes, showing the graphic details of the Hunts' blood loss, were not introduced.

Most of the other pieces of evidence had no clear logical reason for being collected, and if they were tested, no analyses were ever disclosed. For example, the hair samples taken from Jo Ann, Jim Thomas, and the bed were never introduced in court.

Three plaster casts were collected, but only two were used in court. The casts were not labeled as to what they were or where they came from. Why did no one tell the photographer to get pictures of the footprints around the home?

In the Nolan County trial, Dr. Janes explained that he removed the bullet from Roy's skull at the funeral home—the only time the removal of the bullet was mentioned. The bullet was never presented as evidence. What happened to it?

Similarly, the chloroform-soaked rag used to subdue Jo Ann was never noted or presented.

What about the jurors in Jim's cases? Given that only seventeen pieces of evidence were presented, the task of these juries in drawing a guilty conclusion against Jim is hard to imagine.

One of the most difficult tasks in the entire judicial procedure is jury deliberations. Jurors are normally average citizens who must exclusively form an opinion based on the facts presented and discern the creditability of the witnesses. They must weigh and evaluate all the evidence and testimonies. In the end, thirty-six jurors were either influenced by the high emotion of Jim's cases, or they had already decided that he was guilty before stepping into the jury box.

The prosecution relied on the evidence of tennis shoes, footprints, tire tracks, and pieces of string to connect Thomas to these murders. The circumstantial evidence was not substantial enough for the higher court to uphold his convictions. Most notably, the state never established Thomas's motive for the killings.

Other questions will forever remain unanswered: Why were the children not hurt? Why did the killer have chloroform, how did he get it, and why did he use it on Jo Ann rather than just leaving her in the closet?

What was Thomas's true character? Was he a loving father and husband? Did he kill all the people alleged by the Texas Rangers? Furthermore, why would a man with a leg injury climb through a window when he could have used the back door? Why did the Texas Rangers target Thomas as a suspect so quickly? Did they have any evidence that pointed to Thomas? Or was he just a culprit upon whom the police could easily pin the murders?

As the investigation dragged on for months, Gault and Hutson were grasping at straws to pin the murders on Thomas. The state had the burden of establishing his guilt, yet Thomas's trials came down to a guessing game of tennis shoes and pieces of string.

D.A. LaFont admirably played the cards he was dealt. Based on the pitiable crime scene investigation that gave him insignificant items to work with, he did the best he could. The burden was on him to ensure the evidence gathered was properly used in court because he was present at the crime scene. However, here, too, grievous questions arise:

Why were the two bullets from the shooting never used in Billy's trials?

Why was that fatal bullet in the murder case never introduced?

29

AUTHOR'S THOUGHTS

The more research I did, the more questions I raised. Some questions grew like Russian thistles, starting off small and growing over time.

But there's more to this complicated story and murder case than just unanswered questions. It has to do with the chilling personal nature of the crime.

During a writers' meeting in Lubbock and later, over a few phone calls, I discussed the case with an author and former Littlefield resident. She mentioned the theory that what happened to the Hunts was deeply personal. Since then, others have raised similar points. That's when I stepped back and began to formulate my own conclusions about who killed the Hunts, and it was reinforced by hearing Jo Ann's story twice.

People kill for many reasons—lust, love, loathing, robbery. I realized after my discussion and talking to Jo Ann that this crime was personal. It was an intimate attack against Mae. It explains the beating she suffered, the positioning of the panties on her, how she was able to talk to Jo Ann, and the horrifying noises Jo Ann heard from the closet before she was doused with chloroform. It explains why Mae was tied so intricately to Roy and why Roy was murdered.

At the time of the murders, people did not talk about rape or sexual assault. It was taboo to even hint at it. Victims were coerced to remain silent and live as nothing had happened. Only one newspaper story mentioned that Mae may have been sexually assaulted. Investigators immediately pushed aside any notions of rape.

DNA testing and sexual assault kits were decades away, so it was impossible to identify semen from a rapist. The lack of these forensic tools only further helped the investigators in their silence on this motive in this case.

Ignoring the evidence and downplaying the possibility of sexual assault or rape became an unspoken procedure among these investigators. They simply did not know how to deal with it.

Not only was Mae assaulted, she and Roy were likely attacked by someone she knew. The killer knew their home—intimately. They knew where the beds were located in the nursery. They knew the bathroom light was kept on.

They knew about the couple's bedroom doors and the kitchen door remaining open since Roy's attempted murder nearly sixteen months before.

A smaller man climbed through that window into the house, not a two-hundred-pound man with a bad leg. If Thomas's reputation was true, he would not have hesitated a second to kill the girls. The man entering that house knew those girls.

What's more, whoever killed the Hunts seized the cover created by Billy's conviction and Ruth's forthcoming trial. This crime had a prime suspect even before it was committed.

The assailant may have been obsessed with Mae, and likely her death may have been inadvertent. After realizing that he had gone too far, the assailant fled the house, ripping the gate off its hinges.

This person knew the Hunts—quite personally—and they owned a gun.

A cold-blooded killer would not have taken the time to bind the victims so intricately. They would have simply walked into the bedroom, shot Roy and Mae while they slept, killed the girls, and walked away into the night undetected.

From the photographs and limited character descriptions from Jo Ann, Mae was beautiful and her personality most likely charmed almost everyone she met. In a dusty town like Littlefield, Mae's movie-star good looks and elegance stood out.

I realized as I considered all the evidence that her death was not meant to happen. The killer was obsessed with Mae because he had been denied. Perhaps she had denied his advances. Perhaps she had broken off an affair. But the violence of the crime shows the killer wanted her and could not have her.

Who did this? Roy and Mae entertained frequently in their home over their brief life together in Littlefield, but their circle of friends was likely quite small. This killer knew the house and knew the habits of the couple after Roy's attempted murder. He knew the girls. Was he watching Mae, longing for her, every time he was in the house? Did every dinner, lunch, or night of cards inflame is unrequited desire?

If Mae knew the killer, it would explain her lack of screams as she was being attacked. If she knew him, she might have been less concerned for her own safety. She could endure the attack as long as her daughters were safe.

In looking for easy suspects, the investigators missed the most important detail of all: The Hunts knew their killer.

This was personal. Very personal.

ENLIGHTENING THE SHADOWS

Decades of autumns have come and gone since the Hunt murders on October 26, 1943, when a killer hid in the shadows on those dark streets and then left the murdered bodies of a doctor and his wife in his wake.

The ties that had literally bound the couple together began weaving outwardly through the community, symbolically connecting to the court system and eventually to other deaths. The community, along with investigators, was thrown into a state of shocked horror. Other murders across the state and nation made the news, but not like the Hunt murders, which became one of the most controversial murder cases in Texas. Law enforcement faced intense pressure to solve the case.

Time turned out to be of the essence in solving these murders. Conventional wisdom to investigations holds that if a murder is not solved within the first seventy-two hours, the chances of solving the case diminish significantly. Yet as the officers and investigators spent months uncovering evidence, they found nothing substantial enough to hold a conviction.

Investigators in the case were not used to investigating murders of this magnitude. They discounted the possibility that Mae had been sexually assaulted.

Basing part of the Hunt murder case on only two pieces of string and tennis shoes was incomprehensible even in 1943. Botched crime scene management and an investigation that focused on only one suspect left more questions than answers.

As time elapsed, finding those answers—and the true murderer—became more challenging.

The most concrete physical evidence, the bullet that killed Roy, is another significant question. Without it, it was impossible to match it to a murder weapon. The bullet was never introduced in court, and no one testified about the likely caliber of gun used.

But what if the bullet was never recovered from Roy? What if it remained in his skull and was buried with him? Even though the bullet was noted in the evidence log, this seems the only plausible explanation.

The dark shadow created by these murders shrouding Littlefield on that near moonless 1943 October night has never lifted. It lingers over the town like the darkness coming before a West Texas thunderstorm. All that remains are unanswered questions, linked together like a spider web.

Even with no statute of limitations on the murders, any overlooked evidence has been lost to time. But did enough evidence to identity the real killer ever exist?

During my research, I wondered whether all the primary investigators, prosecutors, and judges would have performed a more thorough job had they known their actions would be scrutinized decades later. Would they have acted more ethically? Would they have been more meticulous? Would the rape have made it into their reports?

What if investigators had listened to Jo Ann's account of that night? Would they have worked the case differently? Would jurors still have concluded that Jim Thomas murdered the Hunts?

Family members never received any solid answers about the murders. Could it have been for greed? Was it for revenge? Or was it for lust or love?

In the end, no motive was proved or even theorized. Nor was any clear opportunity shown in Thomas's cases. No substantial circumstantial evidence was ever presented. We are left with only speculation, and speculation often leads to nowhere, with only more and more questions.

Based on my research, law enforcement officials followed their guts instead of the evidence, and in doing so, turned the criminal justice system into a three-ring circus.

Present-day Littlefield is a shadow of its former self. Many once-thriving businesses along Main Street are shuttered. Buildings are abandoned to yesteryear's ghosts. The two thriving hospitals became shells of their former selves when the new modern Littlefield Healthcare Center and Hospital was built in 1979.

Long forgotten are the murders of the past that rocked the small town to its core, causing unrest and uncertainty.

The tiny, decaying brick house in this former quintessential West Texas town where a mother and father lost their lives will forever hold a dark secret. Only the Hunts know who killed them and why.

Justice should have done better by them. The legal process should have never rested in this case, not even when Jim Thomas was murdered.

This crime will forever remain a mystery. Jo Ann and Jane knew their parents only briefly, and Roy and Mae never saw their daughters blossom into incredible women and become mothers and grandmothers.

In the end, all that is left is monumental heartbreak and loss: The loss of the Hunts, of course, but also the loss of justice. The court system failed. It failed the victims, their daughters, their families, and society at large. And in that loss, true justice and the answer of who committed these heinous crimes remain bound in silence.

Roy and Mae Hunt
Jo Ann Hunt Price

Jo Ann and Jane Hunt in the backyard of their Littlefield home.
Jo Ann Hunt Price

AFTERWORD

The Hunt Girls

Jo Ann Hunt died on December 6, 2018. She attended the University of Texas, married a football coach, Ivan Price, in 1958, and taught school for thirty-eight years. They lived in Vernon, Wichita Falls, and Georgia. In the Vernon school system, she taught social studies, math, English, and music in grades four to eight. In 1964, the first year of integration, she taught in Locket, Texas.

At the end of 1964, the couple moved to Rush Springs, Oklahoma, where Jo Ann taught grades two to eight in a school that had many Mennonite students. Jo Ann and her husband lived on a farm and raised dairy and limousine cattle, as well as boxers. They had three children and eight grandchildren. In September 2009, her husband died of a massive heart attack.

Jane Hunt is in her eighties. She attended the University of Texas for a year and a half, and then transferred to North Texas State University, now University of North Texas, to be with her high school sweetheart. In 1961, she attended classes in Hawaii, where she fell in love with the islands. She married James Newth in 1964 and they moved to Cedar Hill, where she taught physical education and health and instructed the drill team.

The couple moved to Arkansas, and for two years she taught at North Little Rock High School, which was famously integrated in 1968 with the help of National Guard troops in 1968. They had their first child in 1970 after moving to Dallas. Jane now helps with her husband's business accounts. They have four children and seven grandchildren. Like her sister, Jane raised boxers, as well as German shepherds.

The Franks Family

Discovering any follow-up information on the Franks family became challenging. The only thing I could locate was that Charles Franks, Mae's father, died in August 1954 and is buried in Houston. Mattie, Mae's mother, died in March 1975 from heart failure at age ninety. Mae's brothers and sister died between 1982 to 2007.

The Newtons

In April 1972, Matilda Newton, Billy's mother, was killed during a house fire in Cameron, Texas that destroyed the home. According to her death certificate, Matilda was confined to her room when the fire broke out, cutting off rescue attempts.

Two years later, Ruth moved to Denton, Texas, and Billy remained in Cameron. The couple officially separated in March 1974. According to court documents, their marriage had become insupportable due to a discord of personalities. The court issued a restraining order against Billy because of his violent and ungovernable temper against Ruth. Ruth could not support herself and requested two thousand dollars in monthly support from the man she had been married to for thirty-nine years. At that time, Billy was worth almost three million dollars. Notably, his assets did not mention a plane, but he did have French cows worth over $354,000.

The divorce was finalized on February 26, 1975. Ruth walked away with a Cadillac, a mobile home, her personal belongings, and $125,000 in cash. She was also awarded $4,500 a month for 180 months, as well as her attorney fees of $25,000.

Not much is known about Ruth in her later years. She served as a registered nurse for forty years. She passed away from cancer on October 16, 1980, in Denton and is buried beside her parents at Citizens Cemetery in Clarendon, Texas.

Billy practiced medicine for at least forty-five years. He purchased the Snyder General Hospital and Clinic in Snyder, Texas, in February 1950 and sold it in April 1952.

He never held a specialty board certification, and his primary field was general surgery. The Texas Medical Board never took any actions against him, and he received no formal complaints or medical malpractice claims.

The Newton Memorial Hospital became the Cameron Community Hospital in 1978.

At age seventy-three, Billy died of a heart attack on June 17, 1982, at his home in Cameron. His health had been declining for a number of months. No elaborate obituary was published in the Cameron paper, despite all he had apparently done for the community. He is buried at Oak Hill Cemetery in Cameron.

Jim Thomas

Jim Thomas is buried at Oakwood Cemetery in Waco, Texas. His son, William James Thomas, committed suicide in August 1966 and is buried in the veteran's cemetery in Houston. He served in the U.S. Coast Guard during World War II. His daughter, Adele Frances Thomas Coble, died in May 2003 and is buried in Oklahoma City.

Hubert Deere

Hubert died at sixty-seven in October 1979 and is buried next to his wife at Highland Cemetery in Durant, Oklahoma.

Maney Gault

Maney died in 1947 at the age of sixty-one. He was remembered by fellow officers as a typical Texas Ranger and for inspiring Rangers who followed him with an admiration and enthusiasm for the Ranger service.

Baxter Honey

Baxter passed away on December 18, 1963, from liver failure. His wife Ida Honey died on August 25, 1943, from tuberculosis.

Norvell Redwine

Norvell returned to Lynn County, serving as sheriff in that county from 1952 to 1964 and then from 1968 to 1974. He died in April 1988 at age 88.

Littlefield Hospital

Roy Hunt's partner at Littlefield Hospital, Dr. Thomas B. Duke, did not live long after the murders. Heart problems claimed his life on December 6, 1943. He had been a doctor in Littlefield since 1929. Roy's friend and colleague, Dr. Fred Janes, purchased their surgical practice and equipment at the hospital in late December 1943.

Reward

The reward for the Hunts' killer was never claimed and was given back to all the donors after Jim Thomas was killed in 1951. Only ten percent of the funds were used to help in the investigation, although there's no record of how they were used. The Texas Rangers closed their files on the murders after his death.

The Hunt Home

The Hunt's house still stands in Littlefield in an arrested state of decay. Over twenty people have owned the house or lived there. It was originally built by Pryor Hammons, who was the undertaker when the Hunts were murdered.

The Veazeys

In May 2011, I looked for the Amarillo address where the Veazey home and garage were located, in a historical district near the original Route 66. After driving in circles around Georgia Street, I met Viola Keller, who was standing in front of her home on the same street. During our conversation, she said she had lived in her house for sixty-four years and didn't know of the Veazeys or any house or garage ever having been at their address.

Sid Veazey did exist. He operated Sid's Garage, a wrecker and winch and service garage for over thirty years and frequently advertised in the Amarillo newspaper. Multiple cancers took his life in August 1953.

The Loyds

Grace Loyd served the remainder of Franklin's two-year sheriff term. She later moved to Dimmitt and taught school. In 1968, the Texas Historical Commission erected a historical marker at Franklin's grave in the Littlefield Cemetery. The marker reads: "Born in Montague County. Taking office as sheriff in 1935, he served with honor until mortally wounded in the line of duty. His widow, Mrs. Grace Owen Loyd, served the remainder of his term. He was the father of 8 children."

Eula Andrew "Andy" Bills

The silent prosecuting attorney, Eula Andrew "Andy" Bills, who assisted D.A. LaFont, became the 64th District Judge in November 1949. Governor Allan Shivers appointed Bills to replace Judge Clarence Russell. Bills became an advocate for the unity of forensics and the law. He said that each side should "achieve unfolding unity" given how medical-legal problems were confronting the courts even back in the 1940s and 1950s. In 1958, Bills was appointed Judge to the 154th District Court for the counties of Lamb, Parmer, and Bailey. He had been a teacher before he took up law. He died in 1967.

Texas Women Jurors Amendment, Proposition 6 (1954)

No women served on any of the juries in the cases related to the Hunt murders because it was against the law. In November 1954, voters approved, by a margin of more than 57 percent, a law allowing women to serve on juries.

The graves of Roy and Mae Hunt gravesite in Lubbock.

Christena Stephens

Jo Ann and Jane Hunt in 2012.

Christena Stephens

Jo Ann, Jane, and Christena Stephens in 2012.

Christena Stephens

ACKNOWLEDGMENTS

Thank you, thank you to all who made this possible. This has been a long journey, and many people have helped in the research and writing of this book.

First and foremost, my deepest gratitude goes to the Hunt family members. Sue Sexton, Roy Hunt's niece, has been the strongest supporter of this book since my presentation at West Texas Historical Association (WTHA) in April 2009. She contacted Bill LaFont to request copies of his father's files. Our trip to Plainview to copy those files will forever remain ingrained in my heart as a good day. Without Sue, I never would have had the opportunity of meeting Jo Ann and Jane. I am humbled. I was able to tell Jo Ann's story of what happened that fateful night. Every time I look at their photos, I hope I have done justice to this tragic story, leaving the murder of their parents unsolved. Nancy Hunt Zimmermann reached out to me through social media. She provided never-before-seen photographs of the Hunt family. Nancy also helped locate first names. A special mention goes to Hank Hunt, who also provided insights into the Hunt family history.

Next, my eternal gratitude is extended to Barry for giving me all the time it took to research, write, and edit this story. Without his support, this book would never have come to fruition.

I am forever grateful for my friends who have been supporters and sounding boards for this research. Ginny Phillips has been there from the beginning, from the first presentation to the completion of this book. Sharla Smalling is an ever-encouraging voice who kept me on my path. Sycily Lattimore provided great feedback over dinners and lunches to give me direction with this vast undertaking. Regrettably, Sycily passed away in May 2015.

Cleo Bales, my late cousin who passed away as 2019 came to a close, helped with our family history regarding the car wreck, as well as her remembrances about Littlefield.

Dr. Fred Rathjen and Brenda Haes are two dear friends who have also since passed. Both offered initial guidance on where to start on this research. Without their early words of encouragement, I would not have been able to continue this long and ever-winding path of writing this book.

My thanks go to June Musick, Annette Bingham, and Mary McGinnis, who provided their insights on the early manuscript and provided immeasurable feedback. My gratitude to Cindy Stocker, who gave final editing comments on the revisions.

I am deeply indebted to Kristine Hall for her editing and insights on the progressing road to the final book. They strengthen this hard story by pulling it together more cohesively. Kristine's fresh eyes improved this story immensely, especially with the ingraining of the oxford comma.

I am appreciative of the new friends made along the way during this research. Mari Nicolson-Preuss, Ph.D., provided unbelievable support when it came to gathering old newspaper articles. Gene Preuss, Ph.D., provided the original crime scene photos. Wes Sheffield became a strong supporter of my work on this story in 2009 after my West Texas Historical Association (WTHA) presentation. John McCollough provided information on newspaper articles and the South Plains Army Air Field. Phyllis Wall retrieved historical information from the Plainview area.

Additional special recognition is extended to Arlene Paschel in all her assistance for the forensic aspects of this research.

Thanks to Jim Brown for reaching out to me, a complete stranger, to help him resolve the mystery around his childhood injury and for Dr. Hunt performing a miraculous operation to save his arm. I am thankful to have learned this insight into Roy's surgical talents through corresponding with Jim.

The best lady I met during this research is Janice Peoples. She went above and beyond to help a complete stranger by providing initial copies of newspaper articles related to Jim Thomas's death. After meeting her in person in Durant, Oklahoma, she was gracious, resourceful, and helpful to me. The world needs more people like her.

I would like to acknowledge Diana Melcher and Corinne Wilchenski, formerly with American Bank of Commerce in Lubbock, Texas, who gave me the opportunity to present at the Lunch and Learn series. From this presentation, an unidentified lady asked this one question: "Why can't you go and get DNA off the bodies?" That one question led me to realize I needed to include the early forensics of this story, which turned into a crucial underlying element to the investigation, the convictions, and the appeals.

This research could not have been accomplished without the tireless efforts of the archivists at various libraries. These archivists located files, made copies, and mailed them to me. The one archivist standing out the most is Brenda McClurkin, C.A., Manuscript Archivist, Special Collections, The University of Texas at Arlington. She researched every angle for holdings related to the Newtons, Jim Thomas, and the Hunt murders. Also, Donaly Brice, formerly at the Texas State Library and Archives Commission in Austin, copied all the appeal records from the Kelley, Thomas, and Newton trials, as well as researched the prison archive books. Mr. Brice also allowed me to photograph the crime photos within the appeals records. Catherine Renschler, Adams County Historical Society, Hastings, Nebraska, provided the newspaper and historical book copies of the Hastings Bank robbery, as well as photographs. The Texas Medical Board in Austin, Texas, also provided information on Billy Newton.

A lot of material in this book was due to Bill LaFont. I am extremely appreciative for Mr. LaFont allowing Sue and me to access and copy his dad's files on the cases of Jim Thomas and the Newtons.

Author Bill Neal was an incredible help to me after my 2009 WTHA presentation. Bill obtained copies of the appeal decisions for all the cases, as well as helped clarify certain questions regarding legal matters for me. He also coached me on how to act and interview the Hunt daughters. He passed away in December 2021. Rick Wardroup, a Lubbock attorney, clarified questions regarding the legal research.

I also would like to recognize WTHA for accepting my 2009 paper proposal, "A Double Murder in a Small West Texas Town." The paper was well-received, with one of the largest audiences in attendance for one session. The paper was later published by WTHA in their 2009 West Texas Historical Year Book, Volume LXXXV. WTHA also accepted my 2011 paper proposal, "Catching a Criminal in Early West Texas" which I presented in April 2011.

Special recognition goes to the late Ray Westbrook, former Lubbock Avalanche-Journal features reporter, for covering the 2009 paper. Without his newspaper article coverage, I never would have met Sue Sexton. He passed away in late 2019.

Frances Cupp, at the Pioneer City County Museum, Sweetwater, Texas, is acknowledged for trusting me to get copies of the bound newspaper articles related to Jim Thomas's Nolan County case. Frances gave me an extended tour of the museum, showing me pieces coming out of the original courthouse. I am grateful to Alan Glasscock at the Swisher County Archives and Museum for giving me a detailed tour of the Swisher County Courthouse, as well as for allowing me to take photographs of the former courthouse. Alan passed away in May 2012.

I would like to acknowledge the district and county clerks who also helped with this research: Patti Neill, District Clerk, Nolan County; Brenda Hudson, County and District Clerk, Swisher County; Carla Cannon, District Clerk Hale County; and Pam Huse, Dawson County District Clerk. Extended thanks go to Carter Schildknecht, District Judge, 106th Judicial District of Texas Dawson County.

Joe B. Davis at the Former Texas Rangers Foundation in Kerrville, Texas, provided me the biography of Maney Gault.

I also thank all the ladies at the mosaic classes at GlassyAlley Art Studio and Gallery, Lubbock, Texas, for their continual encouragement since they found out about this book. They include Susan Raines Luesse, Carrie Lowe, Karla Wardroup, Cat Boucher, and Pauline Mills.

Extended appreciations go to the following people for their words of encouragement: Daisy Palmer, Ph.D., David Murrah, Ph.D., and T. Lindsey Baker, Ph.D. The best words of inspiration came from Paul Carlson, Ph.D. after I ran into him at Barnes and Noble in Lubbock who said, "Just get the damn book done!"

Lastly, I have to acknowledge my four-footed babes, Kymba, Tesla, Azrael, and Castiel. Their presence in my life helped me get through this research and writing. They often made dealing with these horrific murders more bearable because I could reach out to touch them or hug them. Kymba, my Japanese chin, was always by my side when I was compiling research, writing, and editing. Often her tail landed on papers or her snook when she sneezed. Kymba passed in October 2013. Tesla, my Entlebucher, was right there with her, allowing me to utilize her as a second desk to hold a book or a document. She never moved and always waited patiently until I was finished. My heart broke when I lost her suddenly in February 2016, making the final edits of this book even more challenging. Even though Azrael, my German shepherd, came into the process late, her ever-loving eyes have always been watchful, as if she were saying, "I am here for you if you need me," and she was. Her absence in my life has been challenging to cope with since her passing October 2022. Castiel, my newest, always smiling, Entlebucher, has this way of getting on my desk chair behind my back, giving me the support I needed to keep going in this final stretch.

To D, I remember sharing the copies of pages I had photocopied with you from those leather-bound newspaper journals. You got so excited because of your own life falling apart. You invested so much and taught me the foundations of researching at courthouses. It was you who initially instigated the travels to the courthouses to find the files. I am deeply grateful to you because without those original files, I would not have had anything to go on to write that first paper for WTHA. It has been a long endeavor, one that has been trying and rife with life's rollercoaster ride. But with every iteration, with every research discovery, it has been an unbelievable journey that in the end you are always thought of with the highest regards and a smile.

Much appreciation to Cranston Reid Photography for my author photo.

Finally, deep gratefulness goes to Loren Steffy, my publisher with Stoney Creek Publishing. He took a chance on me and on this book. He made my writing stronger. I am forever indebted to Loren. Thank you, thank you.

In my oversight, I might have forgotten you who helped me along the way on this path, and if I did forget to mention you—please accept my sincerest apologies and my gratitude for your contribution.

SOURCE NOTES

Source materials used to research and write this book came from extensive primary and secondary resources and are organized by chapter. Due to the variety of sources, instead of listing them as footnotes in their entirety, these notes feature those sources.

The Hunt Family

Interviews with the Hunt family members were invaluable to my research. The record of Jo Ann's story was edited only for clarity. In addition, I relied on court documents, newspaper archives, family photographs, birth and death certificates, oral histories, and Geo. M. Hunt's book *From Early Days Upon The Plains of Texas Poems, Prose, and Selections* on the Hunt family to document their family history.

Other Families

I tried to contact members of the Newton and Thomas families for this research, but either all the children were deceased or I was unable to locate them. To include their perceptions and remembrances from their parents would have been an added benefit. I did have some luck through the Find a Grave website, which linked me to Jim Thomas's niece, who provided and clarified information about his marriages, children, and siblings.

Names

Until the 1950s, newspapers and court documents often referred to people by their initials only. I made every attempt to discover the first or given name of everyone in this book.

Chapter 1 — Broken Silence

This chapter was written from the oral history interviews I conducted with Jo Ann and Jane Hunt in July 2010 and January 2011.

Chapter 2 — Galveston Seaside

Accounts for this chapter came from newspaper reports and trail transcripts.

Chapter 3 — The Drunk

Newspaper accounts from the *Lubbock Avalanche-Journal*, *The County Wide News,* and the *Clovis News Journal* were utilized for this chapter from April 1937 to March 1938. Leroy Kelley's appeal document was acquired from the Texas State Archives in Austin, Texas, 19162, #421. In addition, I consulted E. P. Scott, *"A History of Lamb County,"* Lamb County Historical Commission (1968).

Chapter 4 — Midnight Meeting

Information came from the Lamb County Grand Jury inquiry into the attempted shooting of Roy, were from the lawyer files of Harold LaFont, which included private investigators' reports. Newspaper articles were referenced as well, primarily the *Amarillo Globe-News*, *Lubbock Avalanche-Journal*, *The County Wide News*, and the *Cameron Daily Herald* from May 1942–October 1943. A diversity of other primary sources was used for this chapter. For foundational information on the Newtons coming from *"Matchless Milam History of Milam County Texas Compiled and Edited by Milam County Heritage Preservation Society A Texas Sesquicentennial Edition,"* Milam County Heritage Preservation Society, Taylor Publishing Company, Dallas, Texas (1984) and L.M. Batte, *"History of Milam County, Texas,"*

The Naylor Company (1956). In addition, I referenced a variety of newspaper archives from the *Amarillo Globe-News, The Evening Herald—Plainview, Lubbock Avalanche-Journal, The County Wide News, Cameron Daily Herald, Fort Worth Star-Telegram,* and the *Dallas Morning News* from May 1942–1948. Other information came from the Smith and Wenig private investigator reports from Harold LaFont's files. Also referenced were the Texas Medical Board, Billy and Ruth Newton's court documents from Lamb, Hale, and Swisher Counties were utilized. Billy's appeal from Lamb County was used from the Texas State Archives, 22679, #609. The weather records were taken from the Weather Bureau, Washington, 1942.

Chapter 5 — Three-Ring Circus

This chapter was written using Billy and Ruth Newton's court documents from Lamb, Hale, and Swisher Counties. Newspaper archives referenced, but were not limited to, included *Amarillo Globe-News, Tulia Herald, The Evening Herald—Plainview, Lubbock Avalanche-Journal,* and *The County Wide News* from 1942–1948. Billy's appeal from Lamb County was used from the Texas State Archives, 22679, #609. The private investigator reports of Smith and Wenig in Harold LaFont's files were also sourced as well.

Chapter 6 — Life Amongst Cottonfields

Literature resources for this chapter included, but were not limited to, the following: L.L. Graves, ed, "*A History of Lubbock,*" West Texas Museum Association on the campus Texas Technological College (1962); D. B. Gracy II, "*Arthur P. Duggan and the Early Development of Littlefield,*" *West Texas Historical Association Year Book,* 64 (1968); V. M. Peterman, "*Pioneer Days: A Half-Century of Life in Lamb County and Adjacent Communities,*" Lubbock: Texas Tech Press (1979); K. E. and C.R. St. Clair, eds., "*Little Towns of Texas,*" Jayroe Graphic Arts, Jacksonville, Texas, (1982); E. P. Scott, "*A History of Lamb County,*" Lamb County Historical Commission (1968); and G. M. Hunt, "*From Early Days Upon The Plains of Texas Poems, Prose, and Selections,*"

A.G. and C.E. Hunt Lubbock, Texas, (1919). I also researched through newspaper archives of *The County Wide News* from 1937 to 1943. The 1940 census was also referenced: **http://1940census.archives.gov/**.

Chapter 7 — Murderer in the Shadows

The murder scene description came from all the Jim Thomas trial transcripts acquired from the Texas State Archives, Austin, Texas. The primary resource materials for this chapter were the Special Collections Library at the University of Texas Arlington, Arlington, Texas. In addition, newspaper accounts from across the United States were utilized, including *Lubbock Avalanche-Journal, Amarillo Globe-News, Kansas City Star, The County Wide News, Chicago Daily Tribune, The Evening Herald—Plainview,* and *The Washington Post* from October 1943 to December 1943. Additionally, Jim Thomas's files and records of Harold LaFont were utilized from Bill LaFont. The weather records were taken from the Weather Bureau, Washington, 1943.

Chapter 8 — Evidence and Funerals

The main newspaper sources were the *Fort Worth Star-Telegram, The County Wide News, Lubbock Avalanche-Journal,* and *the Plainview Evening Herald* from October 1943–December 1944. Hammons Funeral Home body cards were consulted as well. Harold LaFont's files were used to fill in the gaps for this chapter. Trial transcripts of Jim Thomas were referenced for this chapter from Lamb, Hale, Dawson, and Nolan counties. The Oral History of Harold M. LaFont was accessed at the Southwest Collection, Texas Tech University, conducted on June 23, 1998, by Gene B. Preuss. Additionally, the following literature sources were used: C. Fricke, *"Criminal Investigation,"* O.W. Smith Law Books, Los Angeles, CA (1930); R. Wittthaus, *"Medical Jurisprudence, Forensic Medicine and Toxicology,"* (1896); J. Wawesik, "History of chloroform anesthesia," Anaesthesiol un Reanimation, (1997); R. L. Rivers, "Embalming Artifacts," *Journal of Forensic Science* (1978); N.S. Bokarius, "Book Review of External Inspection of the Corpse at the Place of Accident or of Its Discovery," *Kharkoff*

Institute, (1929); "Report on Necropsies," *The New York Academy of Medicine, The New York Pathological Society, and the Metropolitan Funeral Directors' Association,* (1931); The American Journal of Police Science (1930); G. O'Grady, "Death of the teaching autopsy," *BMJ* (2003); and B. Brasol, Book Review, External Inspection of the Corpse at the Place of Accident or of Its Discovery, *The American Journal of Police Science*, (1930).

Chapter 9 — Alibis, Leads, and Rumors

The primary sources for this chapter were *The County Wide News, Lamb County Leader-News, Lubbock Avalanche-Journal,* and *the Amarillo Globe-News* from October 1943–December 1944. References on Maney Gault came from M. Cox, *"Texas Ranger Tales, Stories Need Telling,"* Republic of Texas Press (1997). The Former Texas Ranger Museum in Fredericksburg, Texas, provided biographical information on Gault. Trial transcripts of Jim Thomas were referenced for this chapter from Lamb, Hale, Dawson, and Nolan counties.

Chapter 10 — Sensational Spectacle

For the primary sources for this chapter, see notes for chapters two and three.

Chapter 11 — Rolling Into 1944

A variety of newspaper archives were utilized for this chapter from *Amarillo Globe-News, The County Wide News, Lubbock Avalanche-Journal, Canyon News,* and *Dallas Morning News* in 1944.

Chapter 12 — Who's Jim

Newspaper archives utilized for this chapter were from *Amarillo Globe-News, The County Wide News, Lubbock Avalanche-Journal, Canyon News,* and the *Dallas Morning News* from 1942–1951. Smith and Wenig private investigator reports were utilized from Harold LaFont's files. Texas Prison Archives in Huntsville, Texas was referenced. Court records related to Jim Thomas from McLennan County,

Texas, were utilized. Other foundational research came from the Jim Thomas Lubbock County Assault Case against Baxter Honey, Court Case # 2678. Court records on the Canyon bank robbery were acquired from the Randall County Justice Center. The Hastings Public Library in Hastings, Nebraska, provided copies of newspaper articles and county history files detailing the Hasting's bank robbery. Additionally, Jim Thomas's Federal Bureau of Investigation (FBI) File #245,134 was referenced.

Chapter 13 — Improper Evidence

File 147 Texas Criminal 400, 180, S.W. 2d 946 Texas Court of Criminal Appeals decision on Billy's Lamb County trial was referenced. This information was given to me by Bill Neal. Billy Newton's Appeal from Lamb County, 22679, #609 from the Texas State Archives in Austin, Texas, was referenced. Information from Harold LaFont's records and files pertaining to the Billy and Ruth Newton were used as well.

Chapter 14 — Trials and Shenanigans

The source materials used for this chapter were the Hale and Swisher counties court documents of Billy and Ruth Newton. Additionally, the *Plainview Daily Herald*, *Lubbock Avalanche-Journal*, *The County Wide News*, *Tulia Herald*, and the *Amarillo Globe-News* from 1944–1946 were referenced. The Special Collections Library at the University of Texas Arlington, Arlington, Texas, provided a variety of newspaper articles from various sources. The Swisher County Courthouse record #948 was referenced, along with Billy Newton's appeal record from the Texas State Archives, #23637.

Chapter 15 — Affirmation

The Texas Court of Criminal Appeals decision was referenced in Billy Newton's Swisher County trial 150 Texas Criminal 500, 202, S.W. 2d 921. This information was given to me by Bill Neal. The Swisher County trial transcript was used. Material from Harold LaFont's records and files pertaining to Billy Newton were referenced as well.

Chapter 16 — Circumventing Prison

The source materials for this chapter primarily came from Harold LaFont's records and files pertaining to Billy Newton. The Special Collections Library at the University of Texas Arlington, Arlington, Texas, provided various newspaper articles giving an accounting of the parole board hearing.

Chapter 17 — Prison Walls

This chapter was sourced with the help of a variety of newspaper sources, including *The Tulia Herald, Amarillo Globe-News, Cameron Daily Herald, Fort Worth Star-Telegram, Lubbock Avalanche-Journal, Plainview Daily Herald, The County Wide News,* and *Lamb County Leader-News* from 1946–1948. In addition, I referenced the Texas State Archives for Billy Newton's Swisher County appeal record. The Swisher County court record the State of Texas vs. Billy Newton and Ruth Newton was also referenced #948. The mandate from the Court of Criminal Appeals of Billy Newton's case was cited.

Chapter 18 — Innocent Until Proven Guilty

The source materials used for this chapter included files from the Harold LaFont and primary court documents from Lamb and Hale counties, #620 and #2803, respectively. A variety of newspaper articles referenced are from the *Lamb County Leader-News, Amarillo Globe-News, The County Wide News, The Lubbock Avalanche-Journal,* and *The Plainview Daily Herald* from 1944–1945.

Chapter 19 — Misconduct and Retrying

Sources for this chapter came from a variety of newspaper articles from the *Lamb County Leader-News, Amarillo Globe-News, The County Wide News, The Plainview Daily Herald, The Sweetwater Newspaper, The Lubbock Avalanche-Journal, Dawson County Courier,* and *Lamesa Reporter* from 1944–1945. In addition, the Dawson County courthouse trial documents, #1233 were referenced as well.

Chapter 20 — Insufficient Evidence

Jim Thomas's appeal record from Texas State Archives from the Dawson County trial was referenced for this chapter, 23162, #1233. In addition, I sourced the Texas Court of Criminal Appeals decision on Jim Thomas's Dawson County trial, 148 Texas Criminal 526, 189 S.W. 2d 621 Court of Criminal Appeals, #23162. This information was given to me by Bill Neal.

Chapter 21 — One More Time

Source materials used for this chapter include Jim Thomas's Nolan County courthouse trial documents, #2777. Also referenced were a variety of newspapers from the *Fort Worth Star-Telegram, Dallas Morning News, The Nolan County News, The Sweetwater Reporter, The County Wide News, Lubbock Avalanche-Journal,* and *Amarillo Globe-News* from 1945–1947. The Special Collections Library at The University of Texas at Arlington Library, Arlington, Texas, provided a variety of newspaper copies.

Chapter 22 — Failing a Third Time

For documentation of Jim Thomas's second appeal, the appeal records from Texas State Archives from the Nolan County trial were referenced for this chapter. I referred to the Texas Court of Criminal Appeals decision on Jim's Nolan County trial, 1.150 Texas Criminal 540, 203 S.W. 2d 536 Court of Criminal Appeals of Texas, #23680. This information was given to me by Bill Neal.

Chapter 23 — It's Over

The Special Collections Library at The University of Texas at Arlington Library provided the *Fort Worth Star-Telegram* newspaper copies relating to Jim Thomas's death. Court documents related to the Hubert Deere Case #4049 were obtained from the Bryan County Courthouse in Oklahoma, as well as the *Durant Democrat* and *The Oklahoman.* For more information on Jim's death and on, Deere I sourced the Bryan County Genealogy Library and Archives in Calera, Oklahoma.

Chapter 24 — Criminals and Science

The following literature sources were used for this chapter: J. Edgar Hoover, "Criminal Identification," *The American Journal of Police Science*, 2:1 (1931); H. C. Lee, Forensic Science and the Law, *Connecticut Law Review*, (1993). W.S. Wadsworth. "Post Mortem Examinations," *Journal of Criminal Law and Criminology*, (1910). M. Chavigny, "Tracks of Vehicles," *The American Journal of Police Science*, (1930); F. Watzek, "Searching for and Recording Circumstantial Evidence," *The American Journal of Police Science* (1930); C. C.H. Moriarty, "Taking of Casts of Footprints," *Police Journal* (1932); F.W. Martin, "A Simple Method of Taking Footprints," *Police Journal*, (1936); R. Hanzlick, "Death Registration: History, Methods, and Legal Issues," *Journal of Forensic Science* (1997); R. W. Webster, "Legal Medicine and Toxicology," *W.B. Saunders Company. Philadelphia and London*, (1930); W.S. Wadsworth. "Post Mortem Examinations," *Journal of Criminal Law and Criminology*, (1910); C. Fricke, "Criminal Investigation," *O.W. Smith Law Books, Los Angeles, CA*, (1930); T. Kent, "Fingerprinting Techniques. How the methods of enhancing fingerprints at the crime scene are making a difference to investigators," *Forensic Technology Review*, (2010); Committee on Identifying the Needs of the Forensic Sciences Community, National Research Council, "Strengthening Forensic Science in the United States: A Path Forward," *Document No: 228091*, (2009); Dr. Schwarzacher, "Determination of the Age of Bloodstains," *The American Journal of Police Science*, (1930); J. Streeter and M.M. Bellit, *"The 'Fourth Degree': The Lie Detector,"* (1951); J. Edgar Hoover, "Criminal Identification," *The American Journal of Police Science*, 2:1 (1931); N. Morland, *An Outline of Scientific Criminology*, (1950); S. Smith and J. Glaister, "Recent Advances in Forensic Science," *Philadelphia* (1931); G.A. Mitchell, "Circumstantial Evidence from Hairs and Fibres," *The American Journal of Police Science*, (1930); J.E. Hoover, "The Scientific Crime Detection Laboratory," *The University of Chicago Law Review*, (1943); "Identification of String," *Journal of Criminal Law and Criminology*, (1938); A.P. Wescott, "The Literature of Gunshot Injuries," *The American Journal of Police Science*, (1932); and D. Matheson, "The Technique of the American Detective," *Annals of the American Academy of Political and Social Science,* (1929). Also, the appeal transcripts from the Dawson and Nolan counties of Jim Thomas were referenced. Additional literature consulted was D. Matheson, The Technique of the American Detective, *Annals of the American Academy of Political and Social Science,* (1929); H. Hollien, The Expert Witness: Ethics and Responsibilities, *Journal of Forensic Sciences*; (1990); R. W. Webster, *Legal Medicine and Toxicology, W.B. Saunders Company, Philadelphia and London,* (1930); E. Lindsey, Functions of Grand Jury, *Journal of the American Institute of Criminal Law and* Criminology, (1913); and The Calculograph and its Functions, *Page's Engineering Weekly, The Page Publishing Syndicate, Limited,* (1904).

Chapter 25 — Leads Not Followed

For this chapter, I referenced the private investigators' reports by Smith and Wenig from the Harold LaFont files, as well as previous chapter sourced materials.

Chapter 26 — Forensics and Conjectures

I sourced appeal transcripts of Jim Thomas's trials from Nolan and Dawson counties for this chapter, acquired from the Texas State Archives in Austin, Texas.

Chapter 27 — Silent Witness

Resources for this chapter were the following: C. C. Scott, "Medicolegal Photography," Law Review (1946) and C. W. Fricke, "Criminal Investigation," and *O.W. Smith Law Books, Los Angeles, CA,* (1930). I utilized the appeal transcripts of Jim Thomas' trials from Nolan and Dawson counties, as well as resources from other chapters.

INDEX

V

Vacation Bible School, 11, 15
Vaughn, Deputy Sheriff, 216
Veazey, Alvis, 173, 180, 188, 214–15
Veazey, Eva, 158–59, 162, 186
Veazey, Sid, 92, 96, 97, 157–58, 162, 173, 186–87, 214, 245

W

Wagonseller, Wayne, 138
Walton, Jack, 194, 196
Warren, Emmet, 168
Waters, Raymond, 102, 206
Watson, Ed, 67, 75, 220, 222
Weaver, Buster, 32, 104
Westbrook, Ray, 3

West Texas Historical Association (WTHA), 3
White, Dudley, 102
White, Hugh, 102
White, Joe, 90
White, Sara, 37, 207
Whitmire, Jerome, 102
Williams, Goble, 157
Winn, Elgar, 167
Winn, Virgil, 167
Wood, J. L. Ward, 113

Y

York, C. Frank, 80

Z

Zimmerman, Dennis, 131

ABOUT THE AUTHOR

Christena Stephens is a native Texan who grew up exploring nature on the Llano Estacado. After earning two Master of Science degrees, she started a project to preserve a historical Texas ranch, which sparked her interest in history, research, and writing. She did not intend to be a historian but was mentored by the best Texas historians. Several of her writings have been published in anthologies, along with her photographs. In science and history, truths must be told accurately, and she has made truth and authenticity her mission. She still resides on the Llano Estacado, enjoying sunsets and chance porcupine encounters. She is an ardent advocate of wildlife conservation, and her heart belongs to her dogs.

Looking for your next book?

Check out our other titles,
including audio books, at
StoneyCreekPublishing.com.

*For author book signings, speaking engagements
or other events, please contact us at
info@stoneycreekpublishing.com*

A Member of the Texas Book Consortium

http://stoneycreekpublishing.com

Printed in the USA
CPSIA information can be obtained
at www.ICGtesting.com
JSHW072319300624
65552JS00006B/18